IRISH/ENGLISH
ENGLISH/IRISH
DICTIONARY
AND PHRASEBOOK

Sarah Cooney
MC. WT.

HIPPOCRENE BOOKS
New York

Hippocrene Books Edition, 1992

Published in the United States of America
 by Hippocrene Books, Inc., 171 Madison
Avenue, New York, NY 10016.

For information, contact:
HIPPOCRENE BOOKS, INC.
171 Madison Ave.
New York, NY 10016

ISBN 0-87052-110-1
Printed in the United States of America

Contents

Phrasebook

Introduction

The Irish language, still spoken in the 'Gaeltacht' areas of counties Donegal, Galway, Mayo, Cork and Kerry as a community language, represents the last western outpost of an ancient Iron Age Celtic civilisation which extended before the Christian era from these islands as far as Asia Minor. During the last few centuries of its existence the language has been primarily the vehicle for a rich and varied folk culture, unsurpassed anywhere in western Europe, and from the late 1800s it has also been the focus of a popular revival movement which has resulted in a flourishing modern literature.

The main aim of this dictionary is to assist the learner to improve his spoken Irish - hence the pronunciation guide. However, as the use of international phonetic symbols would prove somewhat daunting for many beginners, a system employing the basic spelling rules of English has been chosen here, and the learner is urged to read the Pronunciation Guide carefully and master the value given to each (group of) letter(s).

While the Irish language has possessed a single modernised spelling for a number of decades now there is, unlike English, no single 'preferred' pronunciation, so that the speech of each Gaeltacht region is equally acceptable. The pronunciation given here is based on that of North Connacht, a dialect previously used with success in other popular courses, and which also stands midway between the other major dialects. The spelling is generally in the standard form, with the result that this will now and then diverge from the recommended pronunciation. On a few occasions when the difference might have proved misleading the regional spelling has been adopted and reference made to the standard spelling also.

Pronunciation Guide

d, t as in English but with tongue pressed against back of upper teeth, e.g. *tá* (taa), *dó* (doe).

j, ch as in English 'jeer, cheer' representing Irish *d, t* in connection with *e, i*, e.g. *deas* (jas), *tír* (chee<u>r</u>).

n as in English 'o*n*ion', representing Irish *n* (<u>n</u>) in connection with *e, i*, e.g. *sinn* (shi<u>n</u>).

N as in English but with tongue pressed against back of upper teeth, representing Irish initial *n-* or elsewhere *-nn-*, e.g. *naoi* (Nee).

n as in English 'need', representing Irish *n* elsewhere, e.g. *dona* (dunu).

<u>l</u> as in English 'million', representing Irish *l* (<u>l</u>) in connection with *e, i*, e.g. *mill* (mi<u>l</u>).

L as in English but with tongue pressed against back of upper teeth, representing Irish initial *l-* or elsewhere *-ll-*, e.g. *lá* (Laa).

l as in English 'leap', representing Irish *l* elsewhere, e.g. *eile* (eli).

r as in English 'foreign', but sounded more forcefully, representing *r, rr* in Irish, e.g. *barr* (baar).

<u>r</u> as in English 'tree', representing Irish *r* in connection with *i, e* other than initially, e.g. *aire* (a<u>r</u>i)

sh as in English 'ship', representing Irish *s* in connection with *i, e*, e.g. *sí* (shee).

s as in English 'sip', representing Irish *s* elsewhere, e.g. *suigh* (see).

<u>**k**</u> as in English 'kin' often followed by brief *y* sound as in 'yes', representing Irish *c* in connection with *i, e*, e.g. *ceo* (<u>k</u>yoe).

k as in English 'Kurd', representing Irish *c* elsewhere, e.g. *cat* (kat).

<u>**g**</u> as in English 'give' often followed by brief *y* sound as in 'yes', representing Irish *g* in connection with *i, e*, e.g. *gearr* (<u>g</u>yaar).

g as in English 'gone' representing Irish *g* elsewhere, e.g. *gob* (gob).

hy as *h* in English 'Hugh, huge', representing Irish *ch* (and sometimes *sh-, th-*) in connection with *i, e*, e.g. *cheol* (hyoel).

kh as in Hiberno-English 'lough' or Scottish English 'loch' and German 'Achtung', representing Irish *ch* elsewhere, e.g. *ach* (akh).

gh a voiced or 'hardened' version of the foregoing, also familiar from German, cf. -g- in 'Tage', representing Irish *dh-, gh-* initially when not in connection with *i, e*, e.g. *dhá* (ghaa).

y as in English 'yes', corresponding to Irish *dh-, gh-* in connection with *i, e* initially, or sometimes internally. It may also be found finally corresponding to y as in English 'Joey', e.g. *a dhlí* (u—ylee), *tráigh* (traa-y).

ng as in English 'sing' or 'song' depending on preceding sound, corresponding to Irish *ng,* e.g. *a ngé* (u—ngae), *a ngabhar* (u—ngoer).

p, b, f, m as in English 'pit, bit, fit, mit', sometimes followed by a *y* sound, e.g. *bó* (boe), *beo* (byoe).

v as in English 'vet' corresponding to Irish *bh, mh* in connection with *i, e,* e.g. *mhill* (vil̠).

w as in English 'wet' corresponding to Irish *bh, mh* elsewhere, e.g. *bhog* (wug).

h as in English 'hot', representing Irish *h, th, sh,* e.g. *hata* (hatu), *both* (boh): note that -h is sounded here vs. *bó* (boe) with long 'o'.

a as in English 'hat', representing Irish *a, ai, ea* in stressed syllables, e.g. *bata* (batu).

aa as in English 'father', representing Irish *á, ái,* e.g. *álainn* (aaLin̠).

e as in English 'deck', representing Irish *e, ei,* e.g. *ceist* (k̠eshch).

ae as in English 'Gael' but one single sound, rather than *e+y,* representing Irish *é, éi, éa,* e.g. *géar* (gyaer).

i as in English 'fit', representing Irish *i, io, ei, ui,* e.g. *giota* (gitu).

o as short version of English *o* in 'wrought, bought' etc., representing Irish *o, oi,* e.g. *cloch* (klokh).

oe as non-standard English pronunciation of *o* in 'stone', i.e. a single sound (not o+oo) representing Irish *ó, ói,* e.g. *dóite* (doe-chi).

u (i) as *u* in English 'chute', representing Irish *o, u* in stressed syllables (normally the first), e.g. *liom* (lum), *rud* (rud);

(ii) as '*u*' in English 'quorum', repre-. senting Irish unstressed vowels, e.g. *agam* (agum).

oo as in English 'too', representing Irish *ú, úi*, e.g. *tú* (too).

ie as in English 'die', representing Irish *aigh-, aidh-*, e.g. *staighre* (stie-r̠i).

ow as in English 'how', representing Irish *amh-*, e.g. *amhaidh* (owlee).

eeu as *ia* in English 'Ian' or standard English *-eer* in 'cheer', representing Irish *ia*, e.g. *grian* (greeun).

aeu as in standard English 'scare' (-r-not sounded), e.g. *ean* (aeun).

oou as *ue* in English 'cruel', representing Irish *ua*, e.g. *fuar* (foour).

Word-stress

As words are normally stressed on the first syllable, there has been no need to mark the stress. Where the stress is irregular a dash has been used to denote that the syllable following this bears the stress, e.g. *amach* (u—makh). As the pronunciation guide given here is English-based a single hyphen is used to separate syllables which familiarity with English spelling might lead one to pronounce as a single syllable, e.g. *staighre* (stie-r̠i), or alternatively to draw attention to separate elements in a sequence of sounds, e.g. *tráigh* (traa-y).

ENGLISH-IRISH
Béarla-Gaeilge

A

able: able to ábalta [aabuLtu]

about (place) timpeall [chimpuL]
  approximately thimpeall is [himpuL is]

above os cionn [as—kyuN]

accident taisme [tashmi]
  I had an accident bhain taisme dom [wan tashmi ghom]

accommodation lóistín [Loeshcheen]

across trasna [trasNu]

after i ndiaidh [i—nae]
  after me i mo dhiaidh [i mu— yae]

age an aois [u—Neesh]

agree: I agree with a person aontaím le duine [eeNteem le dini]

air aer [aeur]

airport aerfort [aerfort]

all uilig [i—log]
  at all ar chor ar bith [xor u bih]

alive beo [byoe]

already cheana féin [hanu faen]

America Meiriceá [merikyaa]

and agus [agus], abbreviated form: is [is]

angry: I am angry with a person tá mé i bhfeirg le duine [ta me i—verig le dini]

animal ainmhí [enivee], otherwise: beithíoch

answer freagra [fragru]

I answer (a person)   tugaim freagra ar dhine [tugim fragru er ghini]

appetite   goile [geli]

April   Aibreán [ebraan]

arm   sciathán [shkihaan]

around   timpeall [chimpuL] (*see also* about)

as: as big as   chomh mór le [khu—moer le]
   as it is   mar atá [mur u—taa]

ashamed: I am ashamed   tá náire orm [ta Naar urum]

ask: I ask for a thing   iarraim rud [eeurum rud]
   enquire   fiarfraim [feeur-heem]

asleep: I am asleep   tá mé i mo chodladh [i mu—xoloo]

at   ag [eg]

August   Lúnasa [Loonusu]

autumn   fómhar [foewur]

awake: I am awake   tá mé i mo dhúiseacht [ta me mo-ghooshukht]

awful   uafásach [ufaasukh]

B

back   (body) druim [drim]
   (direction) ar ais [i—rash]

bacon   muiceoil [mwikyoel]

bad   olc [olk]

bag   mála [maalu]

bald   maol [mweeul]

bank   banc [bangk]

barefoot   costarnocht [kosturNokht]

barrel   baraille [barili]

basin   báisín [baasheen]

basket   ciseán [kishaan], otherwise bascaed

beach trá [traa-y]
beard féasóg [faesoeg]
beautiful álainn [aali_n_]
bed leaba [_l_abee]
bedroom seomra codlata [shoemru koLutu]
bee beach [makh]
beef mairteoil [marchoel]
before: before I go sula dtéim [hulaa`jae-im] (*see also* **front**)
beginning tús [toos]
bell clog [klog], otherwise cloigín
behind (place) ar chúl [e_r_—khool] (motion) ar gcúl [e_r_—gool]
believe: I believe creidim [_kr_ejim]
Belfast Béal Feirste [baeul—fershc_h_i]
below faoi [fwee]
bend: I bend lúbaim [loobim]
   I bend down cromaim síos
bent cam (kam)
beside le taobh [le—teeoo]
besides lena chois sin [lenu khosh shin]
bet geall [_g_yaL]
   I bet a person cuirim geall le duine [Ki_r_im-gyah le-dini]
between idir [ejir]
bicycle rothar [rohur]
big mór [moer]
bird éan [aeun]
black dubh [duv]
blanket pluid [plij]
blind dall [daL]
blow buille [bwi_l_i]
   I blow séidim [shaejim]
blue gorm [gorum]
boat bád [baad]
body corp [korp]
boot buatais [booutish]

both: both boys and girls idir bhuach-
aillí agus chailíní [ejir wokhilee agus
khaleenee]
   you both sibh araon [shiv u—reeun]
bottle buidéal [bwijael]
bottom bun [bun]
   (body) tóin [toen]
bowl babhla [bowlu]
box bosca [bosku]
boy buachaill [bokhil]
break: I break brisim [brishim]
breakfast bricfeasta [brikfastu]
bridge droichead [drehud]
bright geal [gyal]
broad leathan [lahun]
brother deartháir [jrihyaar]
brown donn [duN]
bus bus [bos]
but ach [akh]
buy: I buy ceannaím [kyaNeem]

C

cake císte [keeshchi], otherwise cáca
call glao [glee]
   I call glaoim [glee-im]
car carr [kaar]
care aire [ari]
   I take care of a person tugaim aire
   do dhuine [tugim ari du—ghini]
case (baggage) cása [kaasu]
   (legal) cúis [koosh]
   (general) cás [kaas]
cat cat [kat]
change athrú [arhoo]
   I change athraím [arheem]
   (money) briseadh [brishoo]

chicken cearc [<u>k</u>yark], otherwise sicín
child páiste [paashchi]
cheese cáis [kaash]
choice rogha [row-i<u>n</u>]
choose: I choose toghaim [tow-im]
  church (Roman Catholic) eaglais [aglish]
  (Protestant) teampall [champuL]
Christ Críost [<u>k</u>reest]
Christian Críostaí [<u>k</u>reestee]
Christmas an Nollaig [u—NoLi<u>k</u>]
cigarette toitín [techeen]
clean glan [glan]
  I clean glanaim [glanim]
clear soiléir [silaer]
  (water) glan [glan]
clever cliste [<u>k</u>lishchi]
cliff binn [bi<u>n</u>]
clock clog [klog]
  two o'clock an dó a chlog [u—doe u-khlog]
close: close (to) gar (do) [gar gu]
  I close dúnaim [doonim]
cloth éadach [aedukh]
clothes éadaí [aedee]
cloud néal [<u>n</u>aeul]
coat cóta [koetu]
coffee caife [kafi]
cold fuar [foour]
  I have a cold tá slaghdán orm [ta sLiedaan urum]
  the cold is terrible tá an fuacht uafásach [tan fooukt ufaasukh]
collect: I collect bailím [baleem]
colour dath [dah]
comb cíor [<u>k</u>eeur]
  I comb my hair cíoraim mo cheann [<u>k</u>eerim mu—hyaN]

come: I come tagaim [tagim]
  come in! gabh isteach! [goe ishchak]
  come here! gabh i le! [goe i—le]
comfortable sócúlach [soekoolukh],
  otherwise compórdach
company cuideachta [kijukhtu]
  (business) comhlacht [koelukht]
complain: I complain déanaim gearán
  [jeeunim gyaraan]
completely ar fad [er—fad]
Connaught Connachta [kuNukhtu]
conversation comhrá [koe-raa]
Cork Corcaigh [korkee]
corner coirnéal [kornael]
county contae [kuNdae]
cow bó [boe]
cream uachtar [ooukhtur]
cry: I cry caoinim [keenim]
cup cupán [kopaan]
curtain cuirtín [korcheen]
cut: I cut gearraim [gyarim]

D

damp tais [tash]
dance damhsa [dowsu], otherwise
  rince
danger contúirt [kuNtoorch], otherwise dáinséar
dangerous contúirteach
  [kuNtoorchukh]
dark dorcha [dorukhu]
darkness dorchadas [dorukhudus]
date dáta [daatu]
daughter iníon [ineen]
day lá [Laa]
dead marbh [maroo]

dear (cost) daor [deer]
(beloved) muirneach [mor_nukh]
death an bás [u—baas]
December Mí na Nollag [mee-Nu—
Noluk]
deep domhain [down]
devil diabhal [jowl]
die: I die faighim bás [faam baas]
difference duifear [jifur], otherwise
difríocht
difficult doiligh [delee], otherwise
deacair
difficulty dcacracht [jakrukht]
I am in difficulty tá mé i gcruachás
[ta me i—grooukhaas]
dinner dinnéar [ji_naer]
dining-room seomra bia [shoemru bee]
dirty salach [salukh]
dislike: I dislike a person ní maith liom
duine [_nee mah lum dini]
do: I do déanaim [jeeunim]
doctor dochtúir [dokhtoor]
dog madadh [madoo], otherwise
madra
Donegal Dún na nGall [doo-Nu—
ngaL]
donkey asal [asul]
door dorus [dorus]
doubt amhras [owrus]
I doubt tá mé in amhras [ta me i—
Nowrus]
down (place) thíos [hees]
(motion) síos [shees]
dress gúna [goonu]
I dress (a person) cuirim éadaí (ar
dhuine) [ki_rim aedee i_r ghini]
drink deoch [jokh]
I drink ólaim [ohlim]

drive: I drive tiomáinim [chumaanim]
drizzle ceobhrán [kyoe-wuraan]
drop (liquid) braon [breen]
  I drop leagaim [<u>l</u>agim]
drunk: I am drunk tá mé ar meisce [ta
  me e<u>r</u>—mish<u>k</u>i]
dry tirim [chi<u>r</u>im]
  I dry triomaím [ch<u>r</u>umeem]
Dublin Baile Átha Cliath [blaa kleeu]
dull (weather) gruama [grooumu]
  (subject) neamhshuimiúil [<u>n</u>ow-
  himool]
dumb balbh [baloo]
dust dusta [distu]
during i rith [i—rih]

E

each: each day gach uile lá [khili Laa]
ear cluas [kloous]
early luath [Loou]
Easter an Cháisc [u—khaash<u>k</u>]
eas éascaí [aeskee]
eat: I eat ithim [ihim]
egg ubh [uv]
eight: eight cats ocht gcat [okht gat]
  eight persons ochtar [okhtur]
  (counting) a hocht [u—hokt]
eighth ochtú [okhtoo]
eighty ceithre fichid/scór [<u>k</u>e<u>r</u>i fihyij/
  skoer], otherwise ochtó
electricity aibhléis [avlaesh], otherwise
  leictreachas
eleven: eleven cats aon chat déag [aen
  khat jeeug]
  eleven persons aon duine dhéag [aen
  dini yeeug]

(counting) a haon déag [u—haen
jeeug]

else eile [eli]

empty folamh [foloo]
  I empty folmhaím [foluweem]

end deireadh [jeroo]
  I end (a thing) cuirim deireadh (le
rud) [kirim jeroo le rud]

England Sasana [sasunee]

English Sasanach [sasunukh]
  (language) Béarla [baerLu]
  I speak English tá Béarla agam [ta
baerLu agum]

enjoy: I enjoy (a thing) bainim leas (as
rud) [banim las as rud]

enough go leor [gu—loer]

envelope clúdach litreach [kloodukh
lichrukh]

Europe an Eoraip [u—noerip]

even (surface) réidh [rae]
  even now anois féin [u—Nish haen]

evening tráthnóna [tru—noonu]

ever choíche [kheehu]
  (in past) riamh [u—reeuv]

every: every day gach uile lá [khili Laa]
  everyone gach uile dhuine [khili
ghini]

excellent fíormhaith [feeur-wah]

excuse leithscéal [leshkyael]
  excuse me gabh mo leithscéal [gu
mu—leshkyael]

expensive costasach [kostusukh]

eye súil [sool]

F

face aghaidh [ie-u]

I face (a person) tugaim aghaidh ar dhuine [tugim ie-u er—ghini]

fair féaráilte [faeraalchi]

  fair play cothrom na Féinne [kohrum Nu—faeni]

  fair-haired bán [baan]

fall: I fall titim [chichim]

false bréagach [braegukh]

far: far from i bhfad ó [u—wad oe]

fast sciobtha [shkyopee]

fat ramhar [row-ur]

father athair [ahir]

February Feabhra [fyowru]

feel: I feel mothaím [moheem]

few cúpla [kooplu]

field (crops) gort [gort]

  (pasture) páirc [paark]

fifth cúigiú [koogyoo]

fifty leathchéad [lehyaeud]

fight troid [trej]

  I fight troidim [trejim]

find: I find a thing tagaim ar rud [tagim er rud]

fine (texture) mín [meen]

  (weather) breá [braa]

finger méar [maeur]

finish críoch [kreeukh]

  I finish críochnaím [kreekhneem]

fire tine [chini]

firm daingean [dangyun]

first: the first cat an chéad chat (u—hyeeud khat]

fish iasc [eeusk]

fishing iascaireacht [eeuskirukht]

five: five cats cúig chat [kooig khat]

  five persons cúigear [kooigyur]

flag brat [brat]

floor urlár [orLaar]

flower bláth [bLaa]

fly cuileog [kiloeg]

flying eitilt [echilch]

follow: I follow leanaim [lanim]

following: the following day lá arna mhárach [Laa-urNu-waarukh]

food bia [beeu]

fool (man) amadán [amudaan]
  (woman) óinseach [oenshukh]

foot cos [kos]
  (measure) troigh [trih]

for: I do it for (a person) déanaim do (dhuine é) [jeeunim gu—ghini ae]
  I have been here for a week tá mé anseo le seachtain [ta me in—sho le shakhtin]
  I will be here for a week beidh mé anseo go ceann seachtaine [be me in—sho gu kyaN shakhtini]
  this box is for apples tá an bosca seo le haghaidh úllaí [tan bosku sho le hie ooLee]

forever go deo [gu—joe]

forget: I forget (a thing) déanaim dearmad (de rud) [jeeunim jarumud gu rud]

fork forc [fork]

form cruth [kruh]
  I am in good form tá dóigh mhaith orm [ta doe-y wah urum]

forth: back and forth anonn is anall [u—NuN is u—NaL]

fortnight coicís [kiekeesh]

forty daichead [ghiehyud], otherwise ceathracha

four: four cats ceithre chat [keri khat]
  four persons ceathrar [kyarhur]
  (counting) a ceathair [u—kyahir]

fourth ceathru [<u>k</u>yarhoo]
free saor [seer]
  (gratis) in aisce [i—Nash<u>k</u>i]
friend cara [karu]
friendly cairdiúil [kaarjool]
Friday Dé hAoine [jae—heeni]
from ó [oe]
front tosach [tesukh]
  in front of (place) os comhair [as—
  koe<u>r</u>]
  (motion) roimh [riv]
full lán [Laan]
funny greannmhar [gra<u>N</u>oor]
  odd aisteach [ash<u>ch</u>ukh]
future: in future feasta [fastu]

G

Galway Gaillimh [ga<u>l</u>iv]
gate geata [gyatu]
get: I get fai<u>gh</u>im [faam]
  I get up éirím [ie<u>r</u>eem]
girl cailín [kaleen]
give: I give tugaim [tugim]
glad: I am glad tá lúcháir orm [ta
  Lufaa<u>r</u> urum]
go: I go téim [chae-im]
  I go away imím [imeem]
God Dia [jeeu]
good maith [mah]
goodbye (said to one leaving) slán
  leat/(pl.) libh [sLaan lat/liv]
  (said to one remaining) slán agat/
  (pl.) agaibh [sLaan agut/agiv]
  I say goodbye to someone fágaim
  slán ag duine [faagim sLaan eg dini]
grandfather athair mór [ahi<u>r</u> moer],

otherwise seanathair

grandmother máthair mhór [maahir woer], otherwise seanmháthair

grass féar [faeur]

green glas [glas], otherwise uaithne

grey liath [leeu]

grow: I grow fásaim [faasim]

H

hailstones clocha sneachta [klokhu shnakhtu]

hair gruaig [grooig]

half leath [lah]

half-ton leath-thunna [la-huNu]

halfpenny leathphingin [lafeen]

hand lámh [Laaoo]

happen: it happens to me tarlaíonn sé dom [taarLeen shae ghom]

hard crua [krooi-yi]

hardly: I hardly believe it ní mó ná go gcreidim é [nee moe naa gu—grejim ae]

hat hata [hatu]

hate: I hate someone tá fuath agam do dhuine [ta foou agum gu ghini]

he sé [shae]

head ceann [kyaN]

heart croí [kree]

heavy trom [trum]

hedge claí [klie-u]

hello Dia duit/(pl.) daoibh [jeeu ghich/ yeev]

help cuidiú [kijoo]

I help a person cuidím le duine [kijeem le dini]

hen cearc [kyark]

her í [ee]

    I leave her fágaim í [faagim ee]

    her coat a cóta [u—koetu]

hers: it is hers is léi é [is <u>l</u>aehyi ae]

herself: (she goes) herself (téann) sise [chaen shishi]

    (I see her) herself (feicim) ise [fe<u>k</u>im ishi]

here anseo [i<u>n</u>—sho]

high ard [aard]

hill cnoc [kruk]

him é [ae]

himself: (he goes) himself (téann) seisean [chaen sheshun]

    (I see him) himself (feicim) eisean [fe<u>k</u>im eshun]

his: his coat a cóta [u—khoetu)

    it is his is leis é [is lesh ae]

hit: I hit buailim [booilim]

hole poll [poL]

honey mil [mil]

hope dóchas [doekhus]

    I hope tá súil agam [ta sool agum]

horse capall [kapuL]

hot te [cheh]

hotel teach ósta [chakh oestu]

hour uair [ooi<u>r</u>], uair an chloig [ooi<u>r</u> u—khlig]

house teach [chakh]

how: how are you? cén chaoi a bhfuil tú/(pl.) sibh? [<u>k</u>yaen khee wil too/shiv], otherwise conas?, cad é mar?

    how much/many? cé mhéad? [<u>k</u>yae-vaed]

    how big is it? cé chomh mór agus atá sé? [<u>k</u>yae khu—moer agus taa shae]

    how big it is! nach mór atá sé! [Nukh

moer u—taa shae]

hundred céad [<u>k</u>eeud]

hungry: I am hungry tá ocras orm [ta okrus urum]

husband fear [far]

I

I mé [mae]

ice leac oighre [<u>l</u>ak ie-<u>r</u>i]

if: if (a person is) má (tá duine) [ma ta dini]

if (a person were) dá mbeadh duine [gha me-ukh dini]

ill tinn [chin]

indeed m'anam [manum]

very good ineed an-mhaith ar fad [a<u>n</u>-wah i<u>r</u> f<u>a</u>d]

inside taobh istigh [tee-wi—stih]

interested: I am intererested (in a thing) tá suim (agam i rud) [ta sim agum i—rud]

invitation cuireadh [ki<u>r</u>oo]

invite: I invite a person tugaim cuireadh do dhuine [tugim ki<u>r</u>oo gu—ghini]

Ireland Éirinn [aer<u>in</u>], otherwise Éire

Irish Éireannach [aer<u>u</u>Nukh]

traditional Irish Gaelach [gaelukh]

I speak Irish tá Gaeilge agam [ta gaelgi agum]

is tá [taa]

island oileán [ilaan]

J

January Eanáir [anaar]
jealous: I am jealous (of a person) tá mé ag éad (le duine) [ta me ig aed le dini]
jug crúiscín [krooshkeen]
juice sú [soo]
July mí Iúil [mee ool]
June Meitheamh [mehoo]

K

kettle citeal [kichul]
kind (generous) cineálta [kinaaLtu] (sort) cineál [kinaal]
kill: I kill maraím [mareem]
king rí [ree]
kitchen cistín [kishcheen]
kitten pisín [pisheen]
knife scian [shkeeun]
knock cnag [krag]
  I knock cnagaim [kragim]
know: I know (a thing) tá fhois (agam rud) [ta—is agum rud]
  I know (a place) tá eolas (agam) ar (áit) [ta oelus agum er aach]
  I know a person tá aithne agam ar dhuine [ta anhi agum er ghini]

L

lake loch [Lokh]
lame bacach [bakukh]
land: foreign land tír choimhthíoch [cheer khihee-ukh]

rich land talamh méith [taloo mae]

last deireanach [je_ru_Nukh]

   last night aréir [i—_r_aer]

   last week/year, etc. an tseachtain/
bhliain seo caite [u—chakhtin/vleeun
sho kachi]

late mall [maL] otherwise déanach,
deireanach

law dlí [j_l_eev]

lazy leisciúil [_l_esh_ky_ool]

learn: I learn foghlaimím [fyoelimeem]

leave: I leave fágaim [faagim]

left: left hand lámh chlé [Laaoo hylae]

   on the left ar chlé [e_r_ hylae]

   left behind fágtha [faaku]

leg cos [kos]

Leinster Cúige Laighean [koogi Lie-un]

letter litir [_l_ichi_r_]

lie (falsehood) bréag [b_r_aeug]

   I lie (recline) luím [Lee-im]

life an saol [u—seeul]

light: light coat cóta éadrom [koetu
aedrum]

   bright light solas geal [solus gyal]

   I light the lamp cuirim air an lampa
[ki_r_im e_r_ u—Lampu]

lightning tintreach [chi_n_chukh]

like: like that mar sin [mur—shin]

   like a thing cosúil le rud [kosool le
rud]

   his like a leithéid [u—_l_ehaej]

   I like a person is maith liom duine
[is mah lum dini]

listen: I listen (to) éistím (le) [aesh-
cheem le]

little beag [byog]

   (a) little milk beagán bainne [byo-
gaan ba_n_i]

I understand a little tuigim beagán [chigim byogaan]

live (alive) beo [byoe]

I live here tá mé i mo chónaí anseo [ta me mu—khoenee i̠n—sho]

I live long mairim i bhfad [ma̠rim i—wad]

I live on milk tá mé beo ar bhainne [ta me byoe e̠r wan̠i]

long fada [fadu]

look: I look féachaim [faeukhim], otherwise amharcaim

loose scaoilte [skeel̠chi]

lose: I lose caillim [ka̠lim]

lot: a lot of mórán [moeraan]

loud ard [aard]

love grá [graa]

I love (a person) tá grá agam (do dhuine) [ta graa agum gu—ghini]

lucky: I am lucky tá an t-ádh orm [ta un—taa urum]

lunch lón [Loen]

M

mad: mad dog madadh mire [madoo mi̠ri]

I am mad tá mé ar mire [ta me e̠r mi̠ri]

make: I make déanaim [jeeunim]

man fear [far]

(human being) an duine [u—dini]

manager bainisteoir [banishchoer]

many mórán [moeraan]

marry: I marry pósaim [poesim]

mass (church) an tAifreann [u—taf̠ruN]

(object) meall [maL]
(crowd) slua [sLoou]
match (light) lasóg [lasoeg]
  (game) cluiche [klifi]
matter scéal [shkeeul]
  it doesn't matter is cuma [is—kumu]
  what's the matter? céard atá cearr?
  [kyaerd ta kyaar]
May (month) Bealtaine [baLtini]
  I may féadaim [faedim]
Mayo Maigh Eo [mwee—oe]
me mé [mae]
meat feoil [fyoeil]
memory cuimhne [kivni], otherwise
  meabhair
mend: I mend deasaím [jaseem]
midge míoltog [meeultoeg]
mile míle [meeli]
milk bainne [bani]
mind intinn [inchin]
  I don't mind ní miste liom [nee
  mishchi lum]
mine: it is mine is liom é [is lum ac]
minister (of religion) ministir [minish-
  chir]
  [minish-chir]
minute móiméid [moemaej], otherwise nóiméad
mirror scáthán [scaahaan]
mischievous dána [daanu]
miss (girl) iníon [ineen]
  I miss caillim [kalim]
mist ceo [kyoe]
mistake dearmad [jarumud]
money airgead [arigyud]
month mí [mee]
morning maidin [majin]
  in the morning ar maidin [er majin]
mother máthair [maahir]

mountain sliabh [shleeoo]
mouse luch bheag [Lokh vjog]
mouth béal [baeul]
Munster Cúige Mumhan [koogi moon]
music ceol [kyoel]
mutton caoireoil [keeroel]
my: my milk mo bhainne [mu—wani]

N

naked tarnocht(aí) [taarnokhtee]
name ainm [anim]
narrow cúng [koog]
neck muinéal [mwinaal]
need: I need a thing tá rud uaim [ta rud wem]
never: I never did ní dhearna mé riamh [nee yaarNu mae reeuv]
    I never will do ní dhéanfaidh mé choíche [nee yeenhu mae kheehyi]
new nua [Nooi-yi]
next: the next lesson an chéad cheacht eile [u—hyeeud hyakht eli]
    next door an dara doras [u—dara dorus]
    next week/year an tseachtain/bhliain seo chugainn [u—chakhtin/vleeun sho khogin]
nice deas [jas]
night oíche [eehyi]
    at night san oíche [su—Neehyi]
nine: nine cats naoi gcat [Nee gat]
    nine persons naonúr [Neenoor]
    (counting) a naoi [u—Nee]
ninety ceithre fichid/scór is a deich [keri fihyij is u—jeh], otherwise nócha

ninth naoú [Neeoo]

no: (in answers) repeat verb of question in negative, e.g. an bhfuil tú tinn? [u wil too chin] Níl [neel]
Are you sick? No

no (apples) (ullaí) ar bith [ooLee ur—bih]

nobody duine ar bith [dini ur bih]

noise fuaim [fooim], otherwise torann

none cuid ar bith [kij ir bih]

nor ná [Naa]

nose srón [sroen]

not: I do not understand ní thuigim [nee higim]

I did not understand níor thuig mé [neer hig mae]

not that ní sin [nee shin]

note nóta [Noetu]

notice fógra [foougroo]

I notice (a thing) tugaim (rud) faoi dear(a) [tugim rud fwee jar]

nothing rud ar bith [rud ir bih]

now anois [u—Nish]

nurse banaltra [banuLtru]

O

occasionally corruair [kor-ooir]

October Deireadh Fómhair [jeroo foewir]

office oifig [ifig]

often go minic [gu—minik]

old: he is old tá sé sean [ta shae shan]

old coat seanchóta [shan-khoetu]

on ar [er]

once uair amháin [ooir u—waan]

one: one cat kat u—waan]

one person duine amháin [dini u—waa<u>n</u>]

(counting) a haon [u—haen]

only: only you tusa amháin [tis u—waan]

I only understand this ní thuigim ach seo [<u>n</u>ee higim akh shoh]

open oscailte [oski<u>l</u>chi]

I open osclaím [oskleem]

opinion tuai<u>r</u>im [tooi<u>r</u>im]

or nó [Noo]

orange oráiste [uraashchi]

our: our milk ár mbainne [u—ma<u>n</u>i]

ours: it is ours is linn é [is li<u>n</u> ae]

ourselves: we wash ourselves níonn muid muid féin [<u>n</u>ee-un mwij mwij haen]

we take it ourselves tógann muid muid féin é [toegu<u>N</u> mwij mwij haen ae]

out (place) amuigh [u—mwih]

(motion) amach [u—makh]

outside taobh amuigh [tee-wi-mwih]

over thar [har], *see also* **above**

P

palm bos [bos]

paper páipéar [paapaer]

parliament an Dáil [u—daal]

part cuid [kij]

passport pas [pas]

past: past a house thar theach [har hakh]

days past na laetha atá caite [<u>N</u>u—Laehu ta kachi]

path cosán [kosaan]

patient foighdeach [fwiejukh], otherwise foighneach
  (hospital) othar [ohur]
Patrick Pádraig [paadrik]
  St Patrick's Day Lá le Pádraig [Laa
  li paadrik]
pen peann [paN]
penny pingin [peen]
perfect (excellent) thar barr [har—
  baar]
  (complete) iom lán [umlaan], gan
  locht [gun—Lokht]
perhaps b'fhéidir (go) [baejir gu]
person duine [dini]
piece giota [gitu]
pint pionta [piNtu]
pipe píopa [peepu]
pity trua [trooi-yi]
  what a pity nach mór an trua é
  [Nukh moer u—trooi-yi ae]
  (a person) tá trua agam (do dhuine)
  [ta trooi-yi agam gu—ghini]
plate pláta [plaatu]
play: I play imrím [imreem]
pleasant pléisiúrtha [plaeshoor-hu]
please más é do thoil/(pl.) bhur dtoil é
  [maashae du—hil/u—dil ae]
  (it) pleases (someone) taitníonn (sé
  le duine) [taneen shae le dini]
pocket póca [poeku]
poem dán [daan]
policeman Garda [gaardu]
poor bocht [bokht]
pot pota [pota]
potato fata [fatu], otherwise práta
pray: I pray guím [gee-im]
prayer paidir [pajir]
prefer: I prefer is fearr liom [is faar lum]

president uachtarán [ooukhturaan]
price praghas [pries]
   what price is a thing? cé mhéad atá
   ar rud [kyae vaed u—taa ir—rud]
priest sagart [sagurt]
province: the province (of Ulster)
   Cúige (Uladh) [koog—oloo]
pull tarraingt [tarinch]
   I pull tarraingím [taarneem]
purse sparán [spuraan]
put: I put: cuirim [kirim]

Q

quarter ceathrú [kyarhoo]
queen banríon [baNreen]
quiet ciúin [kyooin]
   be quiet bí i do thost/(pl.) bígí i bhur
   dtost [bee du—host/beegee u—dost]
quite: quite good réasúnta (maith)
   [raesooNtu mah]
   quite! m'anam! [manum]

R

rabbit coinín [kinheen]
radio raidió [rajee-oe]
rain báisteach [baashchukh]
   it is raining tá sé ag cur [ta shae kor],
   otherwise fearthain
raw amh [owh]
read: I read léim [lae-im]
recommend: I recommend molaim
   [molim]
red dearg [jarug]
   red-haired rua [roou]

religion creideamh [<u>kr</u>ejoo]

remember: I remember is cuimhin liom [is kivin lum]

rent cíos [<u>k</u>ees]

   rented house teach suite [chakh sichi]

repair: I repair deasaím [jaseem]

rich saibhir [sevi<u>r</u>]

right ceart [<u>k</u>yart]

   all right ceart go leor [<u>k</u>yart gu—loer]

   right hand lámh dheas [Laaoo yas]

   on the right ar dheis [e<u>r</u>—yish]

ring fáinne [faa<u>n</u>i]

   I ring buailim (clog) [booilim klog]

ripe aibí [apee]

rise: I rise éirím [ie-<u>r</u>eem]

river abhainn [ow-i<u>n</u>]

road bóthar [boe-hur], otherwise bealach mór

roast: I roast rósaim [roe-sim]

   roast (meat) (feoil) rósta [fyoeil roestu]

roof mullach an tí [muLukh u—chee], otherwise díon

room seomra [shoemru]

rough garbh [garoo]

round cruinn [kri<u>n</u>]

rub: I rub cuimlím [kimleem]

ruin: I ruin millim [mi<u>l</u>im]

run rith [rih]

   I run rithim [rihim]

S

sake: (for a person's) sake ar son (duine) [er sun dini]

salt salann [saluN]
same céanna [<u>k</u>eeuNu]
  in the same way mar an gcéanna
  [mur u—geeuNu]
Saturday Dé Sathairn [jae sahur<u>n</u>]
say: I say deirim [je<u>r</u>im]
Scotland Albain [alubin], otherwise
  Alba
school scoil [skel]
schoolchild páiste scoile [paashchi
  skeli]
scream scread [sh<u>k</u>rad]
  I scream screadaim [sh<u>k</u>radim]
sell: I sell díolaim [jeelim]
September Meán Fómhair [maan
  foewi<u>r</u>]
service seirbhís [she<u>r</u>iveesh]
seven: seven cats seacht gcat [shakht
  gat]
  seven persons seachtar [shakhtur]
  (counting) a seacht [u—shakht]
seventh seachtú [shakhtoo]
seventy trí fichid/scór is a deich [ch<u>r</u>ee
  fihyij/skoer is u—jeh], otherwise
  seachtó
shadow scáil [skaal]
shake: I shake croithim [krahim]
  I am shaking tá mé ar crith [ta me
  e<u>r</u>—<u>k</u>rih]
shallow tanaí [tanee]
shape cuma [kumu]
sharp géar [<u>g</u>yaeur]
she sí [shee]
sheep caora [keeru]
shelf seilf [shelf]
shine: the sun is shining tá an ghrian ag
  soilsiú [tan yreeun u LuNroo]
shirt léine [<u>l</u>aeni]

shoe bróg [broeg]

shop siopa [shopu]

short gairid [ga_rij]

show: I show taispeánaim [spaanim]

shower cioth [_kyih]

shy cúthail [kool], otherwise cúthalta

sick tinn [chi_n]

side taobh [teeoo]

similar: similar to cosúil le [kosool le]

sin peaca [pakoo]

sing: I sing deirim amhrán [je_rim oeraan]

singing: I am singing tá mé ag rá amhráin [ta me raa oeraa_n]

singer amhránaí [oeraanee]

sister deirfiúr [j_rehoor]

sit: I sit suim [see-im]

I am sitting tá mé i mo shuí [ta me mu—hee]

sitting-room seomra suite [shoemru sichi]

six: six cats sé chat [shae khat]

six persons seisear [sheshur] (counting) a sé [u—shae]

sixth séú [shae-oo]

sixty trí fichid/scór [ch_ree fihyij/ skoer], otherwise seasca

size méid [mae_j]

skin craiceann [kra_kyuN]

sky spéir [spae_r]

sleep codladh [koLoo]

sleepy: I am sleepy tá codladh orm [ta koLoo urum]

slippery sleamhain [sh_low-in]

slow réidh [rae], otherwise mall, socair

small beag [byog]

smell boladh [balhoo]

I smell (something) cuirim boladh rud éigin [ki_rim balhoo rud e—_ki_nch]

smoke toit [tech]
   I smoke (tobacco) caithim tobac [kahim tu—baku]
snow sneachta [shnakhtu]
   it is snowing tá sé ag cur sneachta [ta shae kur shnakhtu]
soft bog [bog]
sole: my sole bonn mo choise [buN mu—khoshi]
some roinnt [rinch]
   some people daoine áiride [deenee aarhiji]
someone duine éigin [din e—kinch]
something rud éigin [rud e—kinch]
sometimes in amannaí [u—Namu-Nee], otherwise uaireanta
son mac [mak]
song amhrán [oeraan]
soon go luath [gu—Loou]
sore tinn [chin], otherwise nimhneach
soup anraith [anhree]
spectacles spéaclóirí [spaekloeree]
spend: I spend caithim [kahim]
spring earrach [arukh]
   in spring san earrach [su—narukh]
stand: I stand seasaim [shasim]
   I am standing tá mé i mo sheasamh [ta me mu—hasoo]
start tús [toos]
   I start tosaím [teseem]
stay: I stay fanaim [fanim]
stick bata [batu]
   I stick (to a thing) greamaím de rud [grameem gu—rud]
stocking stoca [stoku]
stomach goile [geli]
stone cloch [klokh]
stop: I stop stopaim [stopim]

storm stoirm [ste<u>r</u>im]

straight díreach [jee<u>r</u>ukh]

strange (odd) aisteach [ashchukh]
(foreign) comhthíoch [kihee-ukh]

stranger stráinséar [straa<u>n</u>shaer]

street sráid [sraaj]

string sreangán [srangaan]

strong láidir [Laaji<u>r</u>]

sugar siúcra [shookru]

suit (clothes) culaith [kolee]
  it suits me feileann sé dom [felun
  shae ghom], otherwise oirim, fóirim

sum suim [sim]

summer samhradh [sowroo]
  in summer sa tsaamhradh [su—
  towroo]

sun grian [<u>gr</u>eeun]

sunburn dó gréine [doe <u>gr</u>aeni]

sure cinnte [<u>kin</u>chi]

sweet (taste) milis [milish]
  (candy) milseán [mi<u>l</u>shaan]
  (sound) binn [bi<u>n</u>]

swim: I swim snámhaim [sNaawim]
  I can swim tá snámh agam [ta
  sNaaoo agum]

T

table bord [bord], otherwise tábla

tailor táilliúr [taa<u>l</u>oor]

take: I take tógaim [toe<u>g</u>im], otherwise
  glacaim

talk caint [ka<u>n</u>ch]
  I talk labhraím [Lowreem]

taste blas [blas]
  I taste (a thing) blaisim de rud
  [blashim gu—rud]

tea tae [tae] (Note: t- pronounced here as in English)

teach: I teach teagascaim [chagiskim]

teacher múinteoir [moonchoer]

television teilifís [chelifeesh]

tell: I tell (a person a thing) insím [rud do dhuine) [inshim rud gu—ghini]

temper: I am in a temper tá mé crosta [ta me krostu]

ten: ten cats deich gcat [jeh gat]
    ten persons deichniúr [jinhoor]
    (counting) a deich [u—jeh]

tenth deichiú [jehyoo]

than ná [Naa]

thank: I thank (a person) gabhaim buíochas (le duine) [goe-im bweekhus le dini]
    thanks buíochas

thank you go raibh maith agat/(pl.) agaibh [gu ru—mah agut/agiv]

the an [u]
    the cat an cat [u—kat]
    the place an áit [u—Naach]

that: that thing an rud sin [u—rud shin]

them iad [eeud]

themselves: they go themselves téann siadsan [chaen sheeudsun]
    I see them themselves feicim iadsan [fekim eeudsun]

their: their milk a mbainne [u—mani]
    it is theirs is leo e [is loefu ae]

then: I understand then tuigim mar sin [chigim mur shin]
    then he left ansin d'fhág sé [in—shin daag shae]

there ansin [in—shin]
    there is a man who can do it tá fear ann a dtig leis a dhéanamh [ta far aN

u—jig lesh u yeenoo]

there is John! sin Seán [shin shaan]

they siad [sheeud]

thick tiugh [chuf]

thin tanaí [tanee]

thing rud [rud]

think: I think sílim [sheelim]

  I am thinking tá mé ág smaoineamh [ta me—smweenoo]

third tríú [chreeoo]

  one third trian [chreeun]

thirsty: I am thirsty tá tart orm [ta tart urum]

thirty deich is fiche [jeh is fihyi], otherwise tríocha

this seo [shoh]

though: though (I understand) cé (go dtuigim) [kyae gu—jigim]

thousand míle [meeli]

three: three cats trí chat [chree khat]

  three persons triúr [chroor]

  (counting) a trí [u—chree]

throat scornach [skoerNukh]

through thríd [hreej]

thunder toirneach [tornukh]

Thursday Déardaoin [jaer—deen]

ticket ticéad [chikyaed]

tie: I tie ceanglaím [kyangleem]

time an t-am [u—tam]

  a long time tamall fada [tamuL fadu]

tiny bídeach [bweejukh]

tired: I am tired tá tuirse orm [ta tirshi urum]

to: I give something to a person tugaim rud do dhuine [tugim rud gu—ghini]

  I go to Derry téim go Doire [chaem gu diri]

  to the door go dtín doras [gu jeen dorus]

tobacco tobac(a) [tu—baku]

today inniu [i—<u>n</u>uv]

toe méar coise [maeur koshi]
  big toe ordóg coise [ordoeg koshi]

together (place) i gcuideachta [i—gijukhtu]
  (motion) le chéile [le—hyaeli]

tomorrow amárach [u—maarukh]

tongue teanga [cha-ngee]

tonight anocht [u—<u>N</u>okht]

too: I understand too tuigimse freisin [chig imsu freshin]
  too big rómhór [ro—woer]
  too much an iomarca [u—<u>n</u>umur-kee]

tooth fiacail [feeukil]

toothache daigh fiacal [do eeukul], otherwise tinneas fiacal, déideadh

top barr [baar]

touch: I touch (a person) bainim do (dhuine) [banim gu—ghini]

town baile [blaa]

train traein [traen]

tree crann [kraN]

trip turus [torus]

trouble trioblóid [ch<u>r</u>ubloej]

trousers bríste [<u>b</u>reeshchi]

true fíor [feeur]

truth an fhírinne [u—<u>n</u>eeri̱ni]

Tuesday Dé Mairt [jae—maarch]

turn: I turn iontaím [iNteem], otherwise tiontaím, (t)iompaím

twelfth: the twelfth day an daru lá déag [u—daru Laa yeeug]

twelve: twelve cats dhá chat déag [ghaa khat yeeug]
  twelve persons dhá dhuine dhéag [ghaa ghini yeeug]

(counting) a dó dhéag [u—doe-
yeeug]
twenty fiche [fihyi]
twice dhá uair [ghaa oo<u>i</u>r]
twins cúpla [kooplu]
  one twin leathchúpla [<u>l</u>ah-khooplu]
two: two cats dhá chat [ghaa khat]
  two persons beirt [berch]
  (counting) a dó [u—doe]

U

Ulster Cúige Uladh [koog-oloo]
under faoi [fwee]
understand: I understand tuigim
  [chig<u>i</u>m]
undress: I undress (a person) bainim na
  héadaí (de dhuine) [banim Nu—
  haedee gu—ghini]
unless: unless I go mura dtéim [muru
  jaem]
unlike éagsúil le [aegsool le]
unlucky: I am unlucky tá mí-ádh orm
  [ta mee-aa urum]
up (position) thuas [hoous]
  (motion) suas [soous]
until: until morning go maidin [gu—
  majin]
  until I go go dtí go dtéim [gu-jee
  gu—jaem]
unusual neamhghnáthach [<u>n</u>ow-gh-
  raakh]
us muid [mwij]
use leas [<u>l</u>as], otherwise úsáid
  I use (a thing) bainim leas as rud
  [banim <u>l</u>as as rud]
usual iondúil [uNdool]

V

value luach [Looukh]
vegetables glasraí [glasree]
very: very good an-mhaith [an-wah]
view radharc [rie-urk]
village baile beag [bali byog]
visit cuairt [kooirch]
  I visit a person téim ar cuairt chuig duine [chaem er kooirch eg dini]
voice guth [guf]

W

wait: I wait fanaim [fanim]
walk siúl [shool]
  I walk siúlaim [shoolim]
waken: I waken dúisím [doosheem]
wall balla [baLu]
want: I want a thing tá rud uaim [ta rud wem]
waste: I waste a thing cuirim rud amú [kirim rud u—moo]
wash: I wash ním [neem]
watch (time-piece) uaireadóir [ooiridoer]
  I watch breathnaím [branheem]
water uisce [ishki]
Waterford Port Lairge [port Laarigi]
way bealach [balukh]
we muid [mwij]
weak lag [Lag]
weather aimsir [amshir]
wedding bainis [banish]
Wednesday Dé Céadaoin [jae—kyae-deen]
week seachtain [shakhtin]

welcome fáilte [faalchi]
  I welcome a person cuirim fáilte roimh dhuine [kirim faalchi riv ghini]
wet fliuch [flokh]
what céard? [kyaerd]
  what I see an rud a fheicim [u—rud u—ekim]
wheel roth(a) [rohu]
when cén uair? [kyae-un—ooir]
  when I see nuair a fheicim [Nooir u—ekim]
where cén áit? [kae-un-aach]
  where I see an áit a bhfeicim [u—Naach u—vekim]
which: which girl? cén cailín? [kyaen kaleen]
  which of them? cé acu? [kyae akoo]
  which I see a fheicim [u—ekim]
  which puts a chuireas [u—khiris]
whiskey uisce beatha [ishki bahu]
whisper cogar [kogur]
  I am whispering tá mé ag cogar [ta me—kogur]
white bán [baan]
  white-haired liath [leeu]
who ce? (kyae)
  who puts a chuireas [u—xiris]
whom: whom do you see? cé a fheiceann tú? [kyae ekyuN too]
  whom I see a fheicim [u—ekim]
whose: whose shoe is that? cé leis an bhróg sin? [kyae lesh u—vroeg shin]
  whose shoe it is ar leis an bhróg [ur lesh u—vroeg]
why: why do I put? cén fáth a gcuirim? [kyaen faa u—girim], otherwise cad chuige? cad ina thaobh?
  that is why (I put) sin an fáth (a

gcuirim) [shin u—faa u—girim]
widow baintreach [banchrukh]
   widower baintreach fir [banchrukh
   fir]
wife bean [ban]
wild fiáin [fee-aan]
wind gaoth [gee]
window fuinneog [fwinoeg]
wine fíon [feen]
winter geimhreadh [gevroo]
without gan [gun]
woman bean [ban]
wood (trees) coill [kil]
   (material) adhmad [iemud]
word focal [fokul]
work obair [obir]
   I work oibrím [ibreem]
worried buartha [boourhu]
worth: it is worth a lot is fiú mórán é
   [is fyoo moeraan ae]
write: I write scríobhaim [shkreewim]
wrong cearr [kyaar], otherwise mích-
eart

Y

yard (measure) slat [sLat]
year bliain [bleeun]
   this year i mbliana [i—mleeunu]
   New Year an Bhliain Nua [u—
   vleeun Nooiyi]
yellow buí [bwee]
yesterday inné [i—nae]
yes (general assent) is ea [sha] (Note:
   otherwise the Irish idiom is to repeat
   the main verb of the question in the
   positive or the negative, e.g. An

bhfuil sé tinn? Tá/Níl. Is he sick?
Yes/No.)

yet go fóill [gu foeil]

yon: yon hill an cnoc úd(aí) [u—kruk
oodee]

    yon is the hill siúd an cnoc [shid u—
kruk]

yonder ansiúd [in—shid]

you: you are tá tú (sing.)/ sibh (pl.) [ta
too/shiv]

    I see you feicim thú (sing.)/ sibh (pl.)
[fekim hoo/shiv]

young óg [oeg]

your: your milk do bhainne (sing.)/
bhur mbainne (pl.) [du—wani/u—
mani]

yours: it is yours is leat (sing.)/ libh é
(pl.) [is lat/liv ae]

yourself tusa [tisu]

yourselves sibhse [shivshi]

youth (individual) fear óg [far oeg]
(abstract) an óige [u—Noegi]

IRISH-ENGLISH
Gaeilge-Béarla

A

A [u]   who, which, whom, whose: **an fear a fheicim**   the man whom I see; **an fear a fheiceann**   the man who sees; **an rud a thit**   the thing which fell; **an fear a bhfeicim a mhac**   the man whose son I see

all that: **sin a bhfuil agam**   that is all I have;

his: **a chat**   his cat;

her: **a cat**   her cat; **a húll**   her apple

their: **a gcat**   their cat

ábalta [aabultu]   able to

abhainn [owi<u>n</u>]   river

ábhar [aawur]   matter, reason

ach [akh]   but

ní. . . ach   only

ádh: an t-ádh [u—taa]   good luck

ag [eg]   at

aer [aeur]   sky, air

aerfort [aerfort]   airport

aghaidh [ie-u]   face

agus [agus]   and

aibí [apee]   ripe

Aibreán: Mí an Aibreáin [mee un eb<u>ran</u>]   April

Aifreann: an tAifreann [u—taf<u>ru</u>N]   mass (church)

aimsir [amshi<u>r</u>]   weather

ainm [anim]   name

ainmhí [enivee]   animal

aire [a<u>ri</u>]   care, attention

airgead [arigyud] money; silver
áirid [aarhij] certain, some; otherwise
  áirithe
ais: ar ais [ir—ash] back
aisce: in aisce [i—Nashki] free (gratis)
aisteach [ashchukh] strange, unusual
áit [aach] place
  cén áit? where?
aithne [anhi] knowledge, acquaint-
  anceship
álainn [aalin] beautiful
Albain [alubin] Scotland
am [am] time
 in amannaí sometimes
amach [u—makh] out (motion)
amadán [amudaan] fool (male)
amárach [u—maarukh] tomorrow
amh [owh] raw
amháin [u—waan] one: **duine amháin**
  one man
  only: **mise amháin** only me
amhlaidh [owlee] so, thus
amhrán [oeraan] song
amhránaí [oeraanee] singer
amhras [owrus] doubt
amú [u—moo] to waste
  ag dul amú going to waste
amuigh [u—mwih] out (place)
  taobh a muigh de outside of
an [u(n)] the (sometimes followed by
  t-, e.g. **an t-asal** the donkey, **an
  tsúil** the eye
an- [an] very
  an-mhaith very good
anall [u—NaL] hither
anam: m'anam! [manum] indeed!
ann [aN] there (place)
anocht [u—Nokht] tonight

anraith [anhree] soup
anois [u—Nish] now
anonn [u—NuN] thither
   anonn is anall to and fro
anseo [in—sho] here
ansin [in—shin] there
aois [eesh] age
aon [aen] one
Aoine: Dé hAoine [jae—heeni]: Friday
aontaím [eeNteem] I agree
ar [er] on
ár [u] our
   ár gcat our cat
araon [u—reeun] together
ard [aard] high, loud
aréir [i—raer] last night
asal [asul] donkey
atá [u—taa] who/which is/are
athair [ahir] father
athraím [arheem] I change
   athrú [arhoo] change

B

b', ba [b(u)] was, would be
   ba bheag é it was/would be small
babhla [bowlu] bowl
bacach [bakukh] lame; poor man,
   beggar
bád [baad] boat
baile [blaa] home; town
Baile Átha Cliath [blaa kleeu] Dublin
bainim [banim], **bainim do** I touch
   bainim de I take off, remove
bainis [banish] wedding
bainisteoir [banishchoer] manager
bainne [bani] milk

bairille [barili] barrel
báisín [baasheen] basin
balbh [baloo] dumb
balla [baLu] wall
bán [baan] white, fair-haired
banaltra [banuLtru] nurse
banc [bangk] bank
banríon [baNreen] queen
baol [bweel] danger
barr [baar] top; crop
barúil [barool] opinion
bás [baas] death
bata [batu] stick
beach [makh] bee
beag [byog] small
beagán [byogaan] a little/few
béal [beeul] mouth
Béal Feirste [beeul fershchi] Belfast
bealach [balukh] way
  bealach mór main road
Bealtaine [baLtini] May
Béarla [baeurLu] English (language)
beirt [berch] two persons
beithíoch [behee-ukh] animal,
  pl. **beithígh**
beo [byoe] alive
bhur [u] your (pl.)
  bhur gcat [u gat] your cat
bia [beeu] food
bídeach [bweejukh] tiny
binn [bin] sweet, melodious; cliff
bith: ar bith [ir bih] any
  duine ar bith anyone
  ar chor ar bith at all
bithiúnach [behoonukh] rascal
blaisim [blashim] blaisim de   I taste
blas [blas] taste
bláth [blaa] flower

bliain [bleeun] year
bó [boe] cow
bocht [bokht] poor
bog [bog] soft
boladh [balhoo] smell
bolgam [blogum] mouthful
bonn [buN] **bonn coise** sole of foot
bos [bos] palm of hand
bosca [bosku] box
bóthar [boe-hur] road
braon [breeun] drop
breá [braa] fine, beautiful
breac [brak] speckled; trout
bréag [braeug] lie, falsehood
bréagach [braegukh] false, untrue
bricfeasta [brikfastu] breakfast
brisim [brishim] I break
   briste broken
briseadh [brishoo] change (money)
   ag briseadh breaking
bríste [breeshchi] (pair of) trousers
bróg [broeg] shoe
buachaill [bokhil] boy
buailim [booilim] I hit
buatais [booutish] boot
buidéal [bwijael] bottle
buille [bwili] blow, smack
buíoch [bwee-ukh] grateful
buíochas [bweekhus] thanks
bun [bun] bottom, base
bus [bos] bus

C

caife [kafi] coffee
cailín [kaleen] girl
caillim [kalim] I lose

caint [ka<u>n</u>ch] talk
  ag caint talking
cairdiúil [kaarjool] friendly
cáis [kaash] cheese
Cáisc: an Cháisc [u—khaash<u>k</u>] Easter
caithim [kahim] I spend; I use; I wear;
  I smoke (tobacco)
cam [kam] crooked
caoinim [keenim] I cry
caoireoil [kee<u>r</u>oel] mutton
caora [keeru] sheep
capall [kapuL] horse
cara [karu] friend, relative
carr [kaar] car
cás [kaas] case; situation
cása [kaasu] case (luggage)
cat [kat] cat
cathaoir [kaheer] chair
cé [<u>k</u>yae] who?
céad [<u>k</u>eeud] hundred
  an chéad [u—hyeeud] first
  an chéad chat the first cat
Céadaoin: Dé Céadaoin [jae—kyae-
  deen] Wednesday
ceanglaím [<u>k</u>yangleem] I tie
ceann [<u>k</u>yaN] head; one (thing)
  go ceann tamaill for a while
  i gceann tamaill after a while
céanna [<u>k</u>yaeNee] same
ceannaím [<u>k</u>yaNeem] I buy
cearc [<u>k</u>yark] hen
ceart [<u>k</u>yart] right
ceathair [<u>k</u>yahi<u>r</u>] (counting)
  a ceathair four
ceathrar [<u>k</u>yarhur] four persons
ceathrú [<u>k</u>yarhoo] fourth; a quarter
  an ceathrú cat the fourth cat
céile: a chélle [u—hyaeli] each other

le chéile together
ceithre [ke̲ri] four
  ceithre lá four days
cén [k̲yaen] which?
  cén chearc? which hen?
ceo [k̲yoe] mist
ceobhrán [k̲yoe-wuraan] drizzle
ceol [k̲yoel] music
ceoltóir [k̲yoeLtoer] musician
cheana: cheana féin [hanu faen] already
choíche [kheehyi] ever, never
chomh [khu] as
  chomh maith le sin as good as that
chun [un] to
Ciarraí [k̲eeuree] Kerry
cionn: os cionn [as—k̲yuN] over, above
cinéal [k̲inaal] kind, type, sort
cineálta [k̲inaaLtu] kind, generous
cinnte [k̲inchi] certain, sure
cíor [k̲eeur] comb
cíoraim [k̲eerim] I comb
  cíoraim mo cheann I comb my hair
cíos [k̲ees] rent
  ar cíos to let, rented
ciseán [k̲ishaan] basket
císte [k̲eeshchi] cake
cistín [k̲ishcheen] kitchen
citeal [k̲ichul] kettle
cith [k̲ih] shower
ciúin [k̲yooin] quiet
claí [klie-u] hedge, fence
clé [k̲lae] left
  ar chlé on the left
cliste [k̲lishchi] clever
cloch [klokh] stone
clog [klog] clock; bell
  uair an chloig an hour
  a dó a chlog two o'clock

cluas [kloous] ear
clúdach [kloodukh] cover
  clúdach litreach envelope
cluiche [klifi] game, match
cnag [krag] knock, blow
cnagaim [kragim] I knock
cnoc [kruk] hill
codladh [koloo] sleep
codlaím [koleem] I sleep
cogar [kogur] whisper
coicís [kiekeesh] fortnight
coimhthíoch [kihee-ukh] strange, foreign
coinín [kinheen] rabbit
coinne: i gcoinne [i—gini] for the purpose of
coinneal [kinuL] candle
coirnéal [kornael] corner
comhair: os comhair [as—koer] in front of
comhrá [koe—raa] conversation
  ag comhrá conversing
cónaí [koenee] dwelling
  tá mé i mo chonaí ann I live there
Connachta kuNukhtu] Connaught
contae [kuNdae] country
contúirt [kuNtoorch] danger
contúirteach [kuNtoorchukh] dangerous
cor: ar chor ar bith [xor u bih] at all
Corcaigh [korkee] Cork
corp [korp] body
corr [kor] odd, peculiar; occasional
  corrlá an occasional day
corrach [korukh] unsteady
cos [kos] foot
  le cois in addition to
cosán [kosaan] foothpath, track

cosúil [kosool] **cosúil le** similar to
costarnocht [kosturNukt] barefoot
costasach [kostusukh] expensive
cóta [koetu] coat
  cóta mór overcoat
cothrom [korhum] equal, even
craiceann [krakyuN] skin
crann [kraN] tree
creideamh [krejoo] belief, religion
creidim [krejim] I believe
críochnaím [kreekhneem] I finish
Críost [kreest] Christ
Críostaí [kreestee] Christian
crith [krih], **ar crith** shaking
croí [kree] heart
croithim [krahim] I shake
crua(idh) [krooi-yi] hard
cruachás [kroou-khaas] difficulty, hardship
cruinn [krin] round; accurate
crúiscín [krooshkeen] jug
cruth [kruf] shape
cruthaím [kroheem] I create
cuairt [kooirch] visit
  ar cuairt visiting
cuan [kooun] bay
cuid [kij] part
  mo chuid súile my (own) eyes
cuideachta [kijukhtu] company
  i gcuideachta together (position)
cuidím [kijeem] **cuidím le** I help
cúig [kooig] five
cúigiú [koogyoo] fifth
cúigear [koogyur] five persons
cuileog [kiloeg] fly (insect)
cuimhne [kivni] memory, recollection
cuimhneach [kivnukh] is **cuimhneach liom** I remember

cuimlím [kimleem]   I rub
cuireadh [kiroo]   invitation
cuirim [kirim]   I put
cuirtín [korcheen]   curtain
cúis [koosh]   matter, case, affair
cúl [kool]   back
  ar gcúl   back(wards) (motion)
  ar chúl   behind
culaith [kolee]   suit
cuma [kumu]   shape
  is cuma liom   I don't care
cúng [koog]   narrow
cupán [kopaan]   cup
cúpla [kooplu]   a few; twins
cúthail [kool]   shy

D

dá [daa]   if (with meaning 'would')
daichead [ghiehyud]   forty
daigh: daigh fhiacal [do eeukul]
  toothache
Dáil: an Dáil [u—daal]   Irish Parliament
daingean [dangyun]   firm, secure
dall [daL]   blind
damhsa [dowsu]   dance
  ag damhsa   dancing
dán [daan]   poem
  i ndán   in store, fated
daor [deer]   dear
dara [daru]   second, otherwise **darna**
dáta [daatu]   date
dath [dah]   colour
  a dhath   nothing
de [gu]   from
deacracht [jakrukht]   difficulty

déag [jeeug] -teen
  trí déag thirteen
  trí dhuine dhéag thirteen people
deara: faoi dear(a) [fwee jar], **tugaim**
  faio dear(a) I notice
dearg [jarug] red (not hair)
Déardaoin [jaer-deen] Thursday
dearmad [jarumud] **déanaim dearmad**
  I forget, make a mistake
deartháir [jrihyaar] brother
deas [jas] nice; right
  ar dheis [er—yish] on the right
  ó dheas (to) the south
deasaím [jaseem] I mend
deich [jeh] ten
deichiú [jehyoo] tenth
deichniúr [jinhoor] ten persons
deimhin: go deimhin [gu—jivin]
  indeed
deireadh [jeroo] end, finish
Deireadh Fómhair [jeroo foewir]
  October
deireanach [jeruNukh] last, recent
deirfiúr [jrehoor] sister
deirim [jerim], **deirim le** I say (to)
deis [jesh] means, opportunity
deo: go deo [gu—joe] forever
deoch [jokh] drink
dhá [ghaa] two (not in counting)
Dia [jeeu] God
diabhal [jowl] devil
diaidh: i ndiaidh [i—nae] after
díolaim [jeelim] I sell; I pay
díon [jeen] roof, thatch
dinnéar [jinaer] dinner
díreach [jeerukh] straight
  go díreach right, exactly (so)
díth [jee] need, want

diúlaim [joolim] I suck

dlí(odh) [jleev] law

do [gu] to
   do bhean to a woman
   do [du] your
   do bhean your woman (i.e. wife)

dó: a dó [u—doe] two (in counting)

dó dhéag: a dó dhéag [u—doe yeeug]
   twelve (in counting)

dóchas [doekhus] hope

dochtúir [dokhtoor] doctor

dóigh [doe-y] way, condition

doiligh [delee] hard, difficult

dóim [doe-yim] I burn

doirtim [dorchim] I pour

domhan [down] world

domhain [down] deep

donn [duN] brown

doras [dorus] door

dorcha [dorukhu] dark

dorchadas [dorukhudus] darkness

droch- [drokh-] bad

droichead [drehud] bridge

droim [drim] back

duais [dooish] prize

dubh [duv] black

duifear [jifur] difference

duine [dini] man; person; pl. **daoine**
   [deenee]

dúisím [doosheem] I waken
   tá mé i mo dhúiseacht I am awake

dúnaim [doonim] 1 close

Dún na nGall [dooNu–ngaL]
 Donegal

dusta [distu] dust

E

é [ae] he, him, it
éad [aeud] jealousy
éadach [aedukh] cloth
  éadaí clothes
éadrom [aedrum] light (of weight, colour, flavour)
eagla [aglu] fear
eaglais [aglish] church (Roman Catholic)
éagsúil [aegsool] unlike
éan [aeun] bird
Eanáir: mí Eanáir [mee anaar] January
earrach [arukh] spring (season)
eile [eli] other
Éireannach [aeruNukh] Irish; Irish person
éirím [ie-reem] I rise
  éiríonn le duine a person succeeds
Éirinn [ae-rin] Ireland, otherwise Éire
eisean [eshun] himself
éistím [aeshcheem] éistím le I listen to
  éisteacht hearing
eitilt [echilch] flight
  ag eitilt flying
eolas [oelus] knowledge (of place, subject)
Eoraip: an Eoraip [u—noerip] Europe

F

fad [fad] length
  ar fad altogether
  i bhfad ó far from

fada [fadu] long, far
fadalach [fadulukh] slow
fágaim [faagim] I leave
faighim [faam] I get
fáinne [faani] (finger) ring
fairsing [farshin] plentiful, wide
faoi [fwee] under
fásaim [faasim] I grow
féachaim [faeukhim] I look
  feáchaim le I try
féadaim [faedim] I can
fear [far] man, husband
féar [faeur] grass
féaráilte [faeraalchi] fair, just
fearg [farug] anger
fearr: níos fearr [nees faar] better
fearrde [faarji] the better of (something)
féasóg [faesoeg] beard
feasta [fastu] in future, from now on
feicim [fekim] I see
féidir: b'fhéidir [baejir] perhaps
féin [haen] self; even
  sin féin even that
feoil [fyoeil] meat
fiacail [feeukil] tooth
fiafraím [feeur-heem] I enquire, ask a
  question
fiche [fihyi] twenty
fíor [feeur] true; extremely
  fíormhaith extremely good
fios [fis] knowledge (of thing, event)
  tá fhios (is) agam é I know it
fírinne [feerini] truth
fliuch [flokh] wet
foghlaimím [fyoelimeem] I learn
foghlamt(h)a [fyoelumtee] learned,
  wise

fógra [foougroo] notice
foighdeach [fwiejukh] patient, otherwise **foighneach**
fóill: go fóill [gu—foeil] yet, still
folamh [foloo] empty
folmhaím [foluweem] I empty
fómhar [foewur] harvest, autumn
forc [fork] fork
foscadh [foskoo] shelter
fostaím [fosteem] I hire, employ
Frainc: an Fhrainc [u—rangk] France
fraoch [freeukh] heather
freagra [fragru] answer
freagraím [fragreem] I answer
fréamh [fraeoo] root
freastal [frastul] service, waiting on
fuacht [fooukht] cold (temperature)
fuar [foour] cold
fuath [foou] hate, hatred
fud: ar fud [er—fud] throughout
furasta [furustu] easy

G

gabhaim [goe-im] I take, accept
gabh! go, come
gabhar [gow-ur] goat
gach [gakh] every
(g)ach uile/chuile [khili] every
Gaelach [gaelukh] (traditional) Irish
Gaeilge [gaelgi] the Irish language
Gaillimh [galiv] Galway
gairid [garij] short
gar [gar] **gar do** near (to)
garbh [garoo] rough
Garda [gaardu] policeman
gasúr [gasoor] young boy, otherwise

garsún

geal [gyal] bright, shiny

geall [gyaL] bet, promise

geallaim [gyaLim] I promise

géar [gyaeur] sharp

gearán [gyaraan] complaint

  ag gaearán complaining

gearraim [gyarim] I cut

geata [gyatu] gate

giota [gitu] bit, piece

glac [glak] handful

glacaim [glakim] I receive, take

glan [glan] clean

glanaim [glanim] I clean

glao [glee] call

  glaoim [glee—im] I call

glasraí [glasree] vegetables

gnáth: ba ghnáth [bu—ghraa] **leis** he
  used to

gnáthach [graakh] usual, customary

go [gu] to, till; **go dtí** that (in reported
  speech)

goile [geli] stomach; appetite

gorm [gorum] blue

grá [graa] love

greamaím [grameem] I stick, fasten

greannmhar [graNoor] funny

grian [greeun] sun

gruaig [grooig] hair

guím [gee-im] I pray

gúna [goonu] dress, frock

gur [gur] that (past, reported speech)

guth [guf] voice

H

halla [haLu] hall
hata [hatu] hat

I

í [ee] her, she
iad [eeud] them, they
  iadsan [eeudsun] themselves
iarraim [eeurim] I request, ask for
iasacht [eeusukht] loan
iasc [eeusk] fish
iascaireacht [eeuskirukht] fishing
idir [ejir] between
  idir. . . agus both. . . and
im [im] butter
imím [imeem] I go away, depart
imrím [imreem] I play
inchinn [inhin] brain
iníon [ineen] daughter
inné [i—nae] yesterday
inniu [i—nuv] today
insím [insheem] I tell
intinn [inchin] mind
iontaím [iNteem] I turn
is [is] is, are, etc; and
ise [ishi] herself
isteach [i—shchakh] in(to) (motion)
istigh [i—stih] in(side) (position)
ithim [ihim] I eat

L

lá [Laa] day

labhraím [Lowreem] I speak
lag [Lag] weak
láidir [Laajir] strong
Laighin: Cúige Laighean [koogi Lie-un] Leinster
lámh [Laaoo] hand
lampa [Lampu] lamp
lán [Laan] full
lasóg [Lasoeg] match
le [le] with
leaba [labee] bed
leabhar [lowr] book
leagaim [lagim] I lay; I drop; I knock over
leá [laa-im] I melt
leanaim [lanim] I follow
leath [lah] half
leathan [lahun] broad
leathchéad [lehyaed] fifty
leathphingin [lafeen] halfpenny
léim [laem] leap, jump
léim [lae-im] I read
léimim [laemim] I jump
léine [laenee] shirt
leisciúil [leshkyool] lazy
leithscéal [leshkyael] **gabh mo leith-scéal** excuse me
leor [loer] enough
  go leor enough, plenty
liath [leeu] grey
litir [lichir] letter
loch [Lokh] lake
lóistín [loeshcheen] accommodation
lón [Loen] lunch, provisions
luath [Loou] soon
lúbaim [Loobim] I bend
lúcháir [Lufaar] joy, pleasure
luch: luch bheag [lokh vyog] mouse

luím [Lee-im] I lie
Lúnasa [LooNusu] August

M

má [maa] if
mac [mak] son
madadh [madoo] dog, otherwise
  madra
magadh [magoo] fun, mockery
  ag magadh laughing (at)
maidin [majin] morning
Maigh Eo [mwee—oe] Mayo
Máirt: Dé Máirt [jae—maarch]
  Tuesday
mairteoil [marchoel] beef
maith [mah] good
mála [maalu] bag
mall [maL] late; slow
mar [mur] like
  mar sin [mur—shin] thus, so
  cad é mar a? how?
  mar a as, because; where
márach: lá arna mhárach [LaaurNu
  —waarukh] the following day
marbh [maroo] dead
marbhaim [mareem] I kill
margadh [marugoo] market; bargain
máthair [maahir] mother
máthair mhór [maahir woer]
  grandmother
mé [mae] me, I
méad: cé mhéad? [kyae vaed] how
  much/many?
Meán Fómhair [maan foewir]
  September
méar [maeur] finger

méar coise toe
measartha [masuru] moderate, fair
  go measartha maith fairly good
méid [maej] amount, quantity
Meiriceá [merikyaa] America
meisce [mishki] drunkenness
  ar meisce drunk
Meitheamh [mehoo] June
mí [mee] month
mí-ádh: an míádh [u—mee-aa] ill-
  luck, misfortune
mil [mil] honey
míle [mceli] thousand; mile
milis [milish] sweet
millim [milim] I spoil, ruin
millteach [milchukh] excessive
milseán [milshaan] sweet (candy)
mín [meen] smooth, even
minic [minik] often
ministir [minishchir] minister (religion)
míoltóg [meeuLtoeg] gnat, midge
mire [miri] madness
  ar mire mad
miste [mishchi] **ní miste liom** I don't
  mind
mo [mu] my
mó [moe] more
  ní mó ná (go) hardly
móiméid [moemaej] minute, otherwise
  nóiméad
molaim [molim] I praise
mór [moer] big, great
mórán [moeraan] a lot, many
mothaím [moheem] I feel; I hear
muiceoil [mwikyoel] bacon, pork
muinéal [mwinaal] neck
muirneach [mornukh] dear, beloved

Mumha: Cúige Mumhan [koogi moon]
   Munster
mura [mur(u)] unless
   murar same (past)

N

na [Nu] the (prefixes h- before vowel)
ná [naa] than; nor
   ná. . . ! do not . . !
nach [Nukh] is. . .not?; that. . . not
náire [Naari] shame, disgrace
naonúr [Neenoor] nine persons
naoi [Nee] nine
nár [Naar] was. . . not?; that did. . .
   not
neamhghnáthach [now-ghraakh]
   unusual
néal [naeul] cloud
ní [nee] not; thing
níl [neel] is, am, are not
ním [neem] I wash; I do, make
nimhneach [nivnukh] sore, painful
níor [neeur] did/was. . . not
nó [Noo] or; for, because
   nó go until
Nollaig [NoLik], **an Nollaig** Christmas
   Mí na Nollag December
nóta [Noetu] note
nuair [Nooir], **nuair a** when

O

ó [oe] from; since
ocht [okht] eight
ochtar [okhtur] eight persons

ochtú [okhtoo] eighth
ocras [okrus] hunger
óg [oeg] young
oíche [eehyi] night
oifig [ifi<u>g</u>] office
óige [oegi] youth (abstract)
oighre [ie-<u>ri</u>] **leac oighre** ice
óinseach [oe<u>n</u>shukh] stupid woman, girl
ólaim [oelim] I drink
olc [olk] evil
ordóg [ordoeg] thumb
  ordóg coise big toe
oráiste [oraashchi] orange
os: os cionn [as—kyuN] above
  os comhair [as—koe<u>r</u>] before, in front of (position)
osclaím [oskleem] I open
  oscailte [oski<u>l</u>chi] open(ed)
ospidéal [ospijael] hospital
othar [ohur] patient, sick person

P

Pádraig [paadri<u>k</u>] Patrick
  Lá le Pádraig [Laa li paadri<u>k</u>] St Patrick's Day
paidir [paji<u>r</u>] prayer
páipéar [paapaer] paper
páirc [paar<u>k</u>] field (pasture), park
páiste [paashchi] child
pas [pas] pass(port)
peaca(dh) [pakoo] sin
peann [paN] pen
pingin [pee<u>n</u>] penny
piocaim [pyukim] I pick
pionta [piNtu] pint

píopa [peepu] pipe
pisín [pisheen] kitten
pláta [plaatu] plate
pléisiúrtha [plaeshoor-hu] pleasant, enjoyable
pluid [plij] blanket
póca [poeku] pocket
poll [poL] hole
Port Láirge [port Laarigi] Waterford
pósaim [poesim] I marry
pota [potu] pot
praghas [pries] price
práta [praatu] potato, otherwise **fata**
punt [puNt] pound

R

raidio [rajee-oe] radio
ramhar [row-ir] fat, thick
réasúnta [raesooNtu] reasonable
  réasúnta saor fairly cheap
réidh [rae] even, steady
rí [ree] king
riamh [u—reeuv] ever, never (in past)
rith [rih] run, running
  i rith during
rithim [rihim] I run
ro(-) [ro-] too, excessively
rogha [row] choice
roimh [riv] before
roimhe [u—rivi] previously, before now
roinnt [rinch] some, a number
rósaim [roesim] I roast
  rósta roasted
roth(a) [rohu] wheel
rothar [rohur] bicycle

rua [roou]   red-haired, sandy
rud [rud]   thing

S

sagart [sagurt]   priest
saibhir [sevir]   rich, wealthy
salann [saluN]   salt
samhradh [sowroo]   summer
saor [seer]   cheap; free, unfettered;
   craftsman
Sasana [sasunee]   England
Sasanach [sasunukh]   English; an Eng-
   lishman
Satharn: Dé Sathairn [jae—sahurn]
   Saturday
scáil [skaal]   shadow; reflection
scairt [skarch]   shout
scairtim [skarchim]   I call
scáthán [skaahaan]   mirror
scaoilim [skeelim]   I loose
   scaoilim le   I shoot at
scaoilte [skeelchi]   loose
scéal [shkeeul]   story, subject
scian [shkeeun]   knife
sciathán [shkihaan]   wing; arm
scioabtha [shkyopee]   fast
scoil [skel]   school
scornach [skoernukh]   throat
scread [shkrad]   screech, scream
sé [shae]   six; he, it
seacht [shakht]   seven
seachtain [shakhtin]   week
seachtar [shakhtur]   seven persons
seachtú [shakhtoo]   seventh
seal [shal]   a while, period
sean(-) [shan]   old

seasaim [shasim] I stand
séidim [shaejim] I blow
seilf [shelf] shelf
seirbhís [sheriveesh] service
seisean [sheshun] he himself
seisear [sheshur] six persons
seo [shoh] this (demonstrative)
seomra [shoemru] room
   seomra bia [shoemru bee] dining
   room
   seomra codlata [shoemru koLutu]
   bedroom
   seomra suite [sheomru sichi] sitting-
   room
sí [shee] she
siad [sheeud] they
   siadsan [sheeudsun] they themselves
sibh [shiv] you (pl.)
   sibhse [shivshi] you yourselves (pl.)
sicín [shikeen] chicken
sílim [sheelim] I think, estimate
sin [shin] that (demonstrative)
sinn [shin] we, us
   sinne [shini] we/us ourselves
síos [shees] down(wards) (motion)
sise [shishi] she herself
siúcra [shookru] sugar
siúl [shool] walk
siúlaim [shoolim] I walk
slaghdán [sLie-daan] cold (illness)
slán [sLaan] healthy; whole, complete
   slán leat/agat, etc. goodbye
sleamhain [shlow-in] slippery, smooth
sliabh [shleeoo] mountain
slogaim [sLigim] I swallow
slua [sLoou] crowd, host
sluasaid [sLoousud] shovel

smaoiním [smweeneem] I think, reflect

snámh [sNaaoo] swimming

snámhaim [sNaawim] I swim

snaidhm [sNim] knot

sneachta [shnakhtu] snow

　clocha sneachta [klokhu shnakhtu] hail

sócúlach [soekoolukh] comfortable

soiléir [silaer] visible, clear

soitheach [sehyukh] vessel, dish

solas [solus] light

son: ar son [ur—sun] for, for the sake of

sparán [spuraan] purse

speaclóirí pl. [spaekloeree] spectacles, glasses

spéir [spaer] sky

sráid [sraaj] street

sreangán [srangaan] string

srón [sroen] nose

stoca [stoku] stocking, sock

stoirm [sterim] storm

stopaim [stopim] I stop, halt

stráinséar [straanshaer] stranger

sú [soo] juice, soup

suas [soous] up(wards) (motion)

súil [sool] eye

suim [sim] interest, attention; sum, amount

suím [see-im] I sit

suipéar [sipaer] supper

sul(m)a [hulaa] before (**sul(m)ar** in past)

T

tá [taa]   is, am, are
tábla [taablu]   table, otherwise **bord**
tachtaim [takhtim]   I choke
tae [tae]   tea (Note: t- as in English)
tagaim [tagim]   I come
tailliúr [taaloor]   tailor
tais [tash]   damp
taisme [tashmi]   accident
   de thaisme   by accident
taispeánaim [spaanim]   I show
taitním [taneem] **taitním le duine**
   I please a person
taitneamh [tanoo]   pleasure, enjoy-
   ment
talamh [taloo]   land
tamall [tamuL]   (period of) time, a while
tanaí [tanee]   thin
taobh [teeoo]   side
   le taobh   beside
   taobh istigh/amuigh de   inside/out-
   side of
tarlaím: tarlaíonn sé [taarLeen shae]   it
   happens
tarnocht(aí) [taarnukhtee]   naked
tarraingím [taarneem]   I pull, drag
tart [tart]   thirst
te [cheh]   hot
teach [chakh]   house
teach ósta [chakh oestu]   hotel
teagascaim [chagiskim]   I teach
teampall [champuL]   Protestant church
teilifís [chelifeesh]   television
téim [chae-im]   I go
thar [har]   past, over
thart [hart]   past, by

thíos [hees] down (position)

thrí(d) [hreej] through

thuas [hoous] up (position)

ticéad [chikyaed] ticket

timpeall [chimpuL] around, about
   thimpeall is [himpuL is] approximately

tine [chini] fire

tinn [chin] sick; sore

tiomáinim [chumaanim] I drive

tír [cheer] land, country

tirim [chirim] dry

titim [chichim] I fall

tiugh [chuf] soon, quick

tobac(a) [tu—baku] tobacco

toghaim [towim] I choose

toil [til] will, pleasure
   le do thoil; más é do thoil é (pl. **bhur dtoil**) [le du—hil/maa shae du—hil (u—dil) ae] (if you)please

tóin [toen] backside, bottom

toirneach [tornukh] thunder

toit [tech] smoke

toitín [techeen] cigarette

tormán [torumaan] sound, noise

tosach [tesukh] beginning

tosaím [teseem] I begin

tost [tost] silence
   bí i do thost [bee du host] shut up!

trá(igh) [traa-y] beach

traein [traen] (railway) train

trasna [trasNu] across (motion)

tráthnóna [tru—Noonu] evening, afternoon

treoraím [chroereem] I direct, guide

trí [chree] three

trian [chreeun] one third

trioblóid [chrubloej] worry, trouble

tríú [chreeoo] third (in counting)
triomaím [chrumeem] I dry
troid [trej] fight
troidim [trejim] I fight
troigh [trih] foot (measure)
trom [trum] heavy; dark (colour); strong (flavour)
trua(igh) [trooi-yi] pity
tuairim [tooirim] opinion
tuath [toou] country(side)
tugaim [tugim] I give
tuigim [chigim] I understand
tuilleadh [chiloo] more, an additional amount
tuirse [tirshi] tiredness
turas [torus] trip, journey
tús [toos] beginning
tusa [tisu] you yourself (sg.)

U

uachtar [ooukhtur] cream
uachtarán [ooukhturaan] president
uair [ooir] time, occasion
  cá huair? when?
  uair an chloig hour
uaireadóir [ooiridoer] watch (time-piece)
ubh [uv] egg
uilig [i—log] all
uisce [ishki] water
  uisce beatha [ishki bahu] whiskey
Ulaidh: Cúige Uladh [koogi oloo] Ulster
úll [ooL] apple
úr [oor] fresh; new
urlár [orLaar] floor

IRISH PHRASEBOOK

Notes

In the pronunciation guides the symbol *I* is used to represent the sounds of the Irish *ái* (or *agh* in certain words) and should not be confused with 'I'. For example:

face	**aghaidh**
	Iee
place	**ait**
	Itch

In the translations in this book, the English is set in Roman type, the Irish in bold type, and the guides to pronunciation in italic. For example:

the little window   **an fhuinneog bheag**
                               in inyog vug

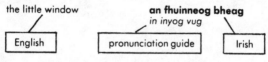

| English | pronunciation guide | Irish |

Contents

Introduction

The purpose of this book is to acquaint visitors, or indeed anyone else with little or no knowledge of Irish, with some of the more common words and phrases currently in use in the language. There is also a brief description of Irish grammar, and this should enable the reader to expand on the phrases given by substituting nouns, persons, adjectives etc. Irish grammar is a difficult subject and a full description of it is outside the scope of this book. The concise description given here, however, should not be off-putting but a useful guide to the reader who wishes to use the phrases given with a greater degree of confidence and accuracy. The aim has been to provide a basis for simple conversation in Irish and to encourage the reader to proceed further on his or her own account and acquire some fluency in the language. The best, if not the only, way to learn a language well is to hear it spoken in its natural setting, and this book may provide an incentive to do just that. Anyone interested in taking the subject a stage further will find numerous books, grammars, dictionaries, etc. easily available, as well as a good selection of tapes, records and other aids. One finds, however, that the average Irish-speaker is the best source of assistance and this is where it is important to be able to ask the right questions.

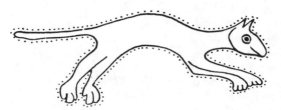

Historical Background

Irish and her sister languages, Welsh and Breton, are among the oldest living languages in Europe. Written records go back to the early Christian period when Latin was often the usual written medium. Irish scribes would sometimes 'gloss' or annotate in the margins of their manuscripts, and it is from these glosses that much of our knowledge of 'Old Irish' has come. Another form of early writing was 'Ogham', consisting of a code of strokes and dots representing the letters, and usually incribed on the edges of upright stones. Hundreds of these 'Ogham Stones' still survive and they usually contain the name of a person, probably as a memorial. They were sometimes erected in honour of dead chieftains or warriors.

Irish developed from one of the Celtic dialects brought to bronze age Ireland and Britain by the iron age Celts, who inhabited Central Europe some three thousand years ago. Ireland was invaded many times and factual evidence is sometimes difficult to obtain. The oral tradition, however, refers consistently to specific events such as 'The Great Plague' and 'The Great Flood' etc. in very factual terms, along-side obviously myth-ological events. Quite often the claims of 'folk history' are corroborated by documentary and other evidence. The invaders of the pre-Celtic period such as Parthalon, Tuatha Dé Danann, Fir Bolg, Milesians, Picts (or Cruithni) are all considered as being ancient inhabitants of Ireland. It can be assumed that when the Celts eventually succeeded in conquering the country that it was a land of many diverse languages, cultures and peoples, even though the population must have been small, and these pre-Celtic languages are thought to have had some influence on what we now call Irish.

Irish was first called 'Gaelic' or 'Goidelic' ('Gaeilge' is the Irish word for the language) by the Welsh. Gaelic mythology and folklore abounds in typically Celtic themes and motifs, such as 'dícheannú' (beheading one's slain enemy) or the 'curadhmhír' (the champion's portion at the feast), as well as many others. Some months of the year are named after pagan Celtic dieties: 'Lúnasa', the month of August, after the god Lugh, as is the town of Lyons in France. There are, of course, hundreds of Irish place-names with Celtic/pagan origins.

The Viking invasions between the eighth and tenth centuries left lasting traces on the culture and language of the population, and many typically Scandinavian words are found in modern Irish, in particular those relating to ships and navigation. The next settlers, the Normans in the twelfth century, brought about a strong French influence, in particular on the literature of the period. Some of the southern dialects of Irish are still detectably influenced by Norman French, and contain several typically French words like 'garsún' (boy).

In the seventeenth century, under English rule, many Irish chieftains and teachers were forced either to emigrate or go into hiding, and for many people education continued only in the illegal 'hedge schools', in fields, barns and sheds. This led to the curious situation where a landlord would address a tenant in English, only to be answered in Greek or Latin. When the first ordnance survey team arrived in Ireland in the early nineteenth century to map the country it enlisted the help of local people, and this team established the anglicised versions of place-names which are in use to-day.

It was also at the beginning of the nineteenth century that scholars, notably Germans, began to unravel the mysteries of 'Old Irish' and Irish studies became a recognized scholarly pursuit. Towards the end of the century the Irish cultural revolution, or 'renaissance', began. Conradh na Gaeilge (The Gaelic League) was founded in 1893 with the principle aim of reviving the Irish language, which was showing signs of decline. There are branches of the Conradh in most towns and these provide excellent classes in Irish at all levels. It is possible that it was only constant pressure from and perseverance of this group that prevented the complete loss of Irish in both the Gaeltacht and in the country as a whole. One of the successes of Conradh na Gaeilge has been the re-establishment of Irish writing as an artistic medium. For about a century Irish writing has been on the increase and the short story has emerged as the medium *par excellence* of this literature. There is also a wide selection of journals, newspapers and magazines available and these are of considerable benefit to learners of the language as well as being a useful vehicle for writers of all types.

Who speaks Irish and where?

The Republic of Ireland, or Eire, is officially a bilingual state with Irish and English having equal status under the law. No-one knows for certain the exact number of Irish-speakers but interest in the language is perhaps as strong now as it has ever been.

The districts in which Irish is still spoken habitually are known as 'An Ghaeltacht' and these are mainly situated on the west coast i.e. in Donegal where 'Ulster Irish' (U), is spoken, in Galway and north Mayo where 'Connacht Irish' (C), is spoken, and in parts of Cork, Kerry and Waterford where 'Munster Irish' (M) is the usual dialect. The Irish used in this book is a composite of the main dialects, based on the so-called 'standard' or official form, the intention being to achieve intelligibility in any part of the country. Regional variations are occasionally given, followed by U, M or C to indicate the dialect concerned or the province in which the variation is normally used.

Pronunciation

The system of pronunciation given in this book is based on normal English spelling. It is impossible to give the exact pronunciation by this method but it does have the advantage of being both simple and intelligible. No attempt should be made to stress the words or syllables in a phrase as stresses and accents vary widely throughout the country. The best method is to speak the words, using the anglicised pronunciation; using this 'neutral' accent you are less likely to go astray. As well as the transliterations, a literal translation is given with some of the phrases and these are indicated by the abbreviation 'Lit.'.

When *t* is followed or preceded by one of the slender vowels *e* or *i* it is usually pronounced like English *ch* as in *chip*. The word *te* (hot), for example, is pronounced *cheh*. When *t* is followed or preceded by one of the broad vowels *a*, *o* or *u* it is pronounced like English *t* (as in *tea*). The tip of the tongue is placed behind the upper front teeth for this sound. When *t* is aspirated, i.e. *th*, it is pronounced like English *h* when it occurs at the beginning of a word, e.g. **mo theach**, *mu hakh* (my house). If it occurs at the end of a word it is always silent, e.g. **fáth** *fa* (a reason) or has an 'h' sound.

The letter *c* in Irish is pronounced like English *k*, e.g. **carr** *kar* (a car). When it is followed by a slender vowel however, (*i* or *e*), it acquires a *ky* sound as in **cearr**, *kyar* (wrong). The sound *ch* is very common in Irish and can sometimes be a source of difficulty for the learner. It is, in fact, a common sound in many languages and can be pronounced like the *ch* in 'Bach' or Scottish 'loch', or like the *gh* in 'lough'. At the end of a word it is sometimes pronounced like a very strong *h* or *hh* as in **teach**, *chakh* or *chahh* (house).

The letter *d* in Irish, when used with a slender vowel, sounds like English *j* e.g. **deoch**, *jukh* (drink), or **díon**, *jeen* (roof). When used with a broad vowel it can be pronounced like English *d*, e.g. **doras**, *darass* (door). When *d* becomes aspirated, i.e. *dh* it sounds like *y*, e.g. **mo dheoch**, *mu yukh* (my drink). When *dh* is used with a broad vowel it sounds approximately like English *g*, but with a slightly 'breathy' quality: **mo dhoras**, *mu garass* (my door).

Sometimes the vowels in Irish are short and sometimes long. The vowel *a*, when short, can be pronounced like English *a* as in 'bat', but when long (*á*) it is pronounced like *aw* or *au* in most dialects. In Ulster it is more like the long *a* in English 'park'.

The vowel *o* is similar to English *u*: **dona**, *dunna* (bad). When the *o* is long (*ó*) it can be represented by *au*, as in **bó**, *bau* (cow).

The vowel *u* is not unlike the English *u* when short, but when long (*ú*) it is pronounced like the English *oo*: **gúna**, *goona* (a dress).

The vowel *e* has several values and many of these will become apparent from the pronunciations given with the phrases. When *e* is long (*é*) it is usually like *ay*: **féar**, *fayer* (grass).

The vowel *i* is like its equivalent in English: **mill**, *mill* (to destroy). If the *i* is long (*í*) it is pronounced like the English *ee*: **sín**, *sheen* (stretch). The symbol I represents the *i* in English words like 'fire', 'spire', 'shine', etc., and it is used to express the sounds of the Irish *ái* or *agh* in certain words: **aghaidh**, *Iee* (a face); **ait**, *Itch* (a place).

Generally, consonants with slender vowels should be spoken with the lips quite close together as in **bean**, *ban* (a woman), **fear**, *far* (a man), **peann**, *pan* (a pen). Consonants with broad vowels (*a, o, u,*) are pronounced with much more rounded lips: **bán**, *bawn* (white), **fada**, *fawda* (long), **punt**, *punt* (a pound).

The digraph *ao* must be given special considera-
tion, as in some parts of the country it comprises a
sound which cannot be readily described in English
phonetics. It is sometimes pronounced like English
ee and sometimes like *ay*, as in **saol**, *seel* or *sayl*
(life). Either of these pronunciations is acceptable.

The consonants *l*, *n* and *r* vary considerably
according to whether they are used with broad or
slender vowels or whether they are single or
double; *l* with a slender vowel is pronounced like
the *l* in English 'bottle'; *l* at the beginning of a word
is pronounced with a *y* sound when followed by a
slender vowel: **liom**, *lyum* (with me), **leat**, *lyat* (with
you); *ll* has a more rounded sound similar to the *ll* in
'brilliant'. The *n* is quite similar to the English *n*
except when it is doubled, *nn*; this sound sometimes
has a nasal quality. When the double consonant is
followed by *e*, or *i*, it acquires a *y* sound: **fáinne**,
fawnya (a ring). When *nn* occurs at the end of a
word it can sometimes have a slight *ng* sound:
binn, *bing* (harmonious). This is a subtle sound and
is only prominent in certain parts of the country.

Both *r* and *rr* are not unlike their English counter-
parts, but there are some differences. *ir* is a most
unusual sound to the ears of most English speakers,
but is easily mastered with a little practice.

The consonant *g* is like English *g*, but when
aspirated it is unlike any sound in English; *gh* is like
a 'breathy' version of *g*, the *h* being quite
noticeable.

The consonants *b*, *m* and *p* change completely when aspirated: *p* becomes *ph*, which sounds exactly like English *f*; *bh* sounds like *v* when followed or preceded by a slender vowel (*e* or *i*). It becomes a *w* sound when it has *a*, *o*, or *u* before or after it; *abh*, *obh*, and *ubh* are pronounced: *aw*, *ow* and *uw* respectively. In some southern dialects the *w* sound may be replaced by *v*. There is considerable regional variation in this respect. When *m* is aspirated (*mh*) it also sounds like *w* or *v*, depending on whether it has a broad or slender consonant alongside it, and is exactly like *b* in this respect.

Grammar

The following notes explain certain points arising from the phrases, while other grammatical points are dealt with as they arise in the text.

Nouns

Nouns in Irish are either masculine or feminine. Here are a few examples of masculine nouns with the article:

the man	**an fear**
	a far
the door	**an doras**
	a darass
the book	**an leabhar**
	a lyower
the floor	**an t-urlár**
	a turlar

Note the use of *t* in front of a vowel: **urlár** (a floor). Also that the *n* is sometimes dropped in everyday speech:

the clock	**an clog**
	a klug
the watch	**an t-uaireadóir**
	a toorador
the cupboard	**an cófra**
	a kofra
the boy	**an buachaill**
	a bookhil
the house	**an teach**
	a chakh
the time	**an t-am**
	an tam
the aeroplane	**an t-eitleán**
	an tetchalan

Now here are a few feminine words:

the woman	**an bhean**
	in van
	(but **bean**: a woman)
the window	**an fhuinneog**
	in inyog (*fh* is silent)
the river	**an abhainn**
	in owan

In the case of feminine nouns beginning with a vowel there is no *t* after the article *an*.

the hour	**an uair**
	in oor
the weather	**an aimsir**
	in Imsher
the shoe	**an bhróg**
	a vrog
the hand	**an lámh**
	a lauw or *lawv* (C, M)

Feminine words beginning with *s* have a *t* placed in front of them when used with *an*, as in:

the week	**an tseachtain**
	a chakhtan
the street	**an tsráid**
	a trlj

Adjectives

The adjective always follows the noun which it describes:

the big house	**an teach mór**
	inchakh more
the long road	**an bóthar fada**
	in bohar fada
(a) nice town	**baile deas**
	bala jass
(a) little dog	**madra beag**
	madra bug (C, M)
	(In Ulster the word
	madadh, *madoo*, is
	used for dog)

Notice that the indefinite article 'a' does not exist in Irish.

If a word is feminine, like those listed above, then the adjective following it is sometimes aspirated. (The Irish word for this is **séimhiú**, *shevoo*, to soften.) This process is also referred to as lenition and is a characteristic of the Celtic languages. Here are some examples of adjectives with feminine nouns:

(a) big woman	**bean mhór**
	ban wore
the big woman	**an bhean mhór**
	in van wore
fine (good) weather	**aimsir mhaith**
	Imsher woih
the little window	**an fhuinneog bheag**
	in inyog vug
(a) big window	**fuinneog mhór**
	fwinyog wore

Here are some more adjectives:

pretty	**dóighiúil**
	doyooil
ugly	**gránna**
	grawna
short	**gairid**
	gurij
fat	**ramhar**
	rawar

thin	**tanaí**
	tanee
high	**ard**
	ard
low	**íseal**
	eeshal
full	**lán**
	lawn
empty	**folamh**
	fuloo
bright	**geal**
	gyal
white	**bán**
	bawn
black	**dubh**
	doo (U), *duv* (C, M)
blue	**gorm**
	gurim
green	**glas**
	glass
yellow	**buí**
	bwee
red	**dearg**
	jareg
red (of hair), ginger	**rua**
	rooa
grey	**liath**
	leea
brown	**donn**
	dun

Prepositions

Irish can be described as a language of prepositions, as opposed to a language like English which is largely 'verbal' by comparison. When a preposition is used with a verb it can totally change the meaning of that verb, or give the verb a new shade of meaning. Irish speakers will often use a preposition and verb phrase in place of a simple verb, e.g. **tá sé ag teacht** he is coming (*taw shay a chakht*), but when a preposition such as **le**, (with) is used then the phrase can have a different meaning entirely (**leat**, pronounced *lyat*, means literally 'with you'):

he agrees with you   **tá sé ag teacht leat**

This can also mean 'he is coming with you'. This type of phrase is extremely common. In the above example the verb **aontaigh** (to agree), could have been used.

Some prepositions cause aspiration or eclipsis of following nouns (eclipsis is more common in the south and aspiration in the north, but in many cases either can be used, the various dialects differing considerably in this respect:

on the wall	**ar an bhalla**
	air a walla (U)
on the wall	**ar an mballa**
	air a malla (C, M)

Both of these are equally correct and can of course be used anywhere by the learner. Likewise 'c' is eclipsed by g = gc; 'd' by 'n' = nd; 'f' by 'bh' = bhf; 'g' by n = ng; 'p' by b = bp; and 't' by d = dt. In each case the eclipsing consonant is the one pronounced.

in the bottle	**sa bhuidéal**
	sa wujell
through the window	**tríd an fhuinneog**
	treej in inyog
with the man	**leis an fhear**
	lesh in yar
under the cup	**faoin chupán**
	fween khupan
with the woman	**leis an bhean**
	lesh in van
at the door	**ag an doras**
	eg a darass
on the ground	**ar an talamh**
	air a taloo
past the house	**thar an teach**
	har a chakh
under the chair	**faoin chathaoir**
	fween khaheer
in my pocket	**i mo phóca**
	i mu foca
come from the fire	**tar ón tine**
	tar owin chinee

Here is a list of prepositions:

at	**ag**
	eg
out (of)	**as**
	iss
towards/to	**chuig**
	hig
from/off/of	**de**
	de
to/for	**do**
	dau
along with	**fara**
	farra
under	**faoi**
	fwee
between	**idir**
	idder
in	**i**
	i (as in 'hid')
with	**le**
	le
on	**ar**
	air
before	**roimh**
	riv
past	**thar**
	har
through	**trí**
	tree
from	**ó**
	o (as in 'bone')
round about	**um**
	umm

These prepositions do not always have an exact English equivalent. They are more often found in combination with the personal pronouns (you, me, her, etc.) and the more important of these will be encountered later. Here is an example:

before	**roimh**
	riv
before me	**romham**
	rowam
before you	**romhat**
	rowat

before him/it	**roimhe**
	riva
before her/it	**roimpi**
	rimpee
before us	**romhainn**
	roween
before you (pl.)	**romhaibh**
	rowiv
before them	**rompu**
	rumpoo

Here is another important one:

on	**ar**
	air
on me	**orm**
	urram
on you	**ort**
	urt
on him/it	**air**
	air
on her/it	**uirthi**
	urhee
on us	**orainn**
	ureen
on you (pl.)	**oraibh**
	uriv
on them	**orthu**
	urhoo

It can be seen from this that the endings for the prepositional pronouns form fairly regular patterns.

Plurals

There are several ways of forming plurals in Irish, despite attempts at standardization and, daunting though it may sound, it is probably best to learn each plural as it arises. The method of forming plurals often varies from district to district but this should not be a problem as the root-word generally remains recognizable. Here are a few common examples:

the men	**na fir**
	na fir

the women	**na mná**
	na m-naw (C, M),
	na mra (U)
a person	**duine**
	dinna
the people	**na daoine**
	na deenee
the houses	**na tithe**
	na teeha
a tree	**crann**
	kran
the trees	**na crainn**
	na krin
a light	**solas**
	sulass
the lights	**na solais**
	na sulish
a river	**abhainn**
	owen
the rivers	**na haibhneacha**
	na hivnakha

(Note that the article 'the' changes from 'an' to 'na' in the nominative plural.)

Personal pronouns

I	**mé**
	may
you	**tú**
	too
he	**sé**
	shay
she	**sí**
	shee
we	**muid**
	mij
you (pl.)	**sibh**
	shiv
they	**siad**
	sheead

These are sometimes used with their emphatic or strong form. This is given in brackets. All nouns in Irish can have this emphatic form under certain circumstances, e.g. expression of ownership.

me	**mé, (mise)**
	may, (misha)
you	**tú, (tusa)**
	hoo, (tussa)
him	**é, (eisean)**
	ay, (eshan)
her	**í, (ise)**
	ee, (isha)
us	**muid, (muidinne)**
	muj, (mujinya)
you (pl.)	**sibh, (sibhse)**
	shiv, (shivsha)
them	**iad, (iadsan)**
	eead, (eeadsan)

When used with a verb (for example **tá**, to be) personal pronouns in the nominative case are as follows:

I am	**tá mé**
	taw may
you are	**tá tú**
	taw too
he/it is	**tá sé**
	taw shay
she/it is	**tá sí**
	taw shee
we are	**táimid**
	tawmij
you (pl.) are	**tá sibh**
	taw shiv
they are	**tá siad**
	taw sheead

Verbs

The verb **tá** (to be) is used to express a state or condition, but the verb **is** (to be), pronounced *iss*, must be used when expressing existence and with certain other concepts, e.g.:

he is big	**tá sé mór**
	taw shay more
he is here	**tá sé anseo**
	taw shay inshaw
he is a man	**is fear é**
	iss far ay
he is a big man	**is fear mór é**
	iss far more ay

Is is used in many other structures as well e.g. **is maith liom é** (I like it). The distinction between **is** and **tá** must be closely observed. Many learners of Irish sometimes say, for example, **tá sé teach** for 'it is a house'. The structure **tá sé teach** does not exist in Irish. One can, however, say **tá sé ina theach**, literally 'it is in its state of being a house'.

Is, in conjunction with **le**, is used to express ownership, e.g. **is liom é** (it is mine). This literally means, 'it is with me'.

the coat is yours	**is leat an cóta**
	iss lyat in kota
the money is ours	**is linn an t-airgead**
	iss linn in tarigad
the bicycle is his	**is leis an rothar**
	iss leis in ruhar
they own the place	**is leo an áit**
	iss law in itch
they are yours (pl.)	**is libh iad**
	iss liv eead
the shoes are hers	**is léi na bróga**
	iss leyh na brauga
the house is John's	**is le Seán an teach**
	iss le shan in chakh
who owns the book?	**cé leis an leabhar?**
	kay lesh in lyower
it isn't mine	**ní liom é**
	nee lyum ay
is this your hat?	**an leat an hata seo?**
	un lyat in hata shaw
no (it is not)	**ní liom**
	nee lyum
yes (it is)	**is liom**
	iss lyum

The negative of **is** is **ní**, and the interrogative, or question form, is **an**:

is it a glass?	**an gloine é?**
	in glinya ay
yes (it is)	**is ea**
	sha
no (it is not)	**ní hea**
	nee ha

Fortunately, there are few irregular verbs in Irish and these also happen to be the most commonly used of all the verbs. They are as follows:

make (or do)	**déan**
	jan
come	**tar**
	tar
hear	**clois**
	klish
see	**feic**
	feck
go	**téigh**
	chey
give	**tabhair**
	towar
get	**faigh**
	fI
say	**abair**
	abber
take, (bear, bring or give birth)	**beir**
	beyr
to eat	**ith**
	ih

Most of these verbs will be encountered again later in the book, as will the other points mentioned in this section. One point to bear in mind about the irregular verbs is that they nearly all have dependant forms. These are used in asking questions, in the negative and in reported speech. Here, for example, is the verb **tá** in the present, past, future, conditional and habitual tenses, using the personal pronoun **mé**. Any of the other personal pronouns could be used instead. There are several other tenses in Irish, but these are less likely to be encountered:

I am	**tá mé** (U), **táim** (C, M)
	taw may (U), *tawim* (C, M)
I will be	**beidh mé**
	bay may
I was	**bhí mé**
	vee may

(Note: **tá** is the present tense form of the substantive verb **bí**. **Tá mé anseo** = I am here (now); **bím**

anseo = I am (usually) here.)

I am	**bím**
	beem
I am not	**níl mé**
	neeil may
I will not be	**ní bheidh mé**
	nee vay may
I was not	**ní raibh mé**
	nee row may
I would not be	**ní bheinn**
	nee veyeen
I am not	**ní bhím**
	nee veem
am I?	**an bhfuil mé**
	un will may
will I be?	**an mbeidh mé**
	un may may
would I be?	**an mbeinn?**
	un mayeen
am I?	**an mbím**
	un meem
was I?	**an raibh mé?**
	un row may

Reported speech is simply saying what someone else said:

he said that...	**dúirt sé go...**
	dooart shay gu...
he said that he was ill	**dúirt sé go raibh sé tinn**
	dooart shay gu row shay chin

or with **deir** (to say):

he says that...	**deir sé go...**
	jer shay gu...
he says that he will be here	**deir sé go mbeidh sé anseo**
	jer shay gu may shay un-shaw

and in a negative form:

he says that I was not in the house	**deir sé nach raibh mé sa teach**
	jer shay nakh row may sa chakh

Numbers

Numerals in Irish are as follows:

one	**aon**	*ayn*
two	**dó**	*dau*
three	**trí**	*tree*
four	**ceathair**	*kehar*
five	**cúig**	*kooig*
six	**sé**	*shay*
seven	**seacht**	*shakht*
eight	**ocht**	*okht*
nine	**naoi**	*nee*
ten	**deich**	*jeykh*
eleven	**aon déag**	*aynjeg*
twelve	**dó dhéag**	*dauyeg*
thirteen	**trí déag**	*treejeg*
fourteen	**ceathair déag**	*keharjeg*
fifteen	**cúig deag**	*kooigjeg*
sixteen	**sé déag**	*shayjeg*
seventeen	**seacht déag**	*shakhtjeg*
eighteen	**ocht déag**	*okhtjeg*
nineteen	**naoi déag**	*neejeg*
twenty	**fiche**	*fiha*
thirty	**tríocha**	*treeakha*

forty	**daichead**
	dlhad
fifty	**caoga**
	kayga
sixty	**seasca**
	shaska
seventy	**seachtó**
	shakhto
eighty	**ochtó**
	okhto
ninety	**nócha**
	nokha
one hundred	**céad**
	keyd

When used adjectivally, some of these numbers differ slightly. There are several counting systems in Irish, although the following is the simplest and best known:

one pound	**punt amháin**
	punt awoin
two pounds	**dhá phunt**
	dau funt
three pounds	**trí phunt**
	tree funt
four pounds	**ceithre phunt**
	kerra funt
five pounds	**cúig phunt**
	kooig funt
six pounds	**sé phunt**
	shay funt
seven pounds	**seacht bpunt**
	shakht bunt
eight pounds	**ocht bpunt**
	okht bunt
nine pounds	**naoi bpunt**
	nee bunt
ten pounds	**deich bpunt**
	jeykh bpunt
eleven pounds	**punt déag**
	punt jeg
twelve pounds	**dhá phunt déag**
	dau funt jeg
thirteen pounds	**trí phunt déag**
	tree funt jeg

fourteen pounds	**ceithre phunt déag**
	kerra funt jeg
fifteen pounds	**cúig phunt déag**
	kooig funt jeg
sixteen pounds	**sé phunt déag**
	shay funt jeg
seventeen pounds	**seacht pbunt déag**
	shakht bunt jeg
eighteen pounds	**ocht bpunt déag**
	okht bunt jeg
nineteen pounds	**naoi bpunt déag**
	nee bunt jeg
twenty pounds	**fiche punt**
	fiha punt
twenty-one pounds	**punt is fiche**
	punt iss fiha
twenty-two pounds	**dhá phunt is fiche**
	gau funt iss fiha
thirty pounds	**tríocha punt**
	treeakha punt
forty pounds	**daichead punt**
	dlhad punt

Counting people is slightly different yet again:

one person	**duine amháin**
	dinna awoin
one man	**fear amháin**
	far awoin
one girl	**cailín amháin**
	kalleen awoin
two people	**beirt**
	berch
two men	**beirt fhear**
	berch ar
three people	**triúr**
	troor
three women	**triúr ban**
	troor ban
four people	**ceathrar**
	kehrar
four boys	**ceathrar gasúr**
	kehrar gasoor
five people	**cúigear**
	kooigar

five men	**cúigear fear**
	kooigar far
six people	**seisear**
	sheshar
six women	**seisear ban**
	sheshar ban
seven people	**seachtar**
	shakhtar
seven children	**seachtar páiste**
	shakhtar pashtee
eight people	**ochtar**
	okhtar
eight fools	**ochtar amadán**
	okhtar amadaun
nine people	**naonúr**
	neenoor
nine sailors	**naonúr mairnéalach**
	neenoor marnyalakh
ten people	**deichniúr**
	jeynoor
eleven people	**duine déag**
	dinna jeg
twelve people	**beirt déag**
	berch jeg

Common Words and Phrases

how are you?	**cad é mar atá tú?**
	kajay mara ta too (U)
how are you?	**cén chaoi a bhfuil tú?**
	keng khee awill too (C)
how are you?	**conas tá tú?**
	kunas taw too (M)
I'm fine, thanks	**tá go maith, go raibh maith agat**
	taw gu mah, gura mah ugut
good-bye	**slán leat** (if you are staying)
	slawn lyat
good-bye	**slán agat** (if you are leaving)
	slawn ugut
good-day, hello	**Dia duit**
	jeea ditch

the reply to this is:	**Dia's Muire duit** *jeeass mwurra ditch*
goodnight	**oíche mhaith** *eeha wah*
what time is it?	**cad é an t-am?** *kajay un tam*
it is five o'clock	**tá sé a cúig a chlog** *taw shay a kooig a khlug*
big	**mór** *more*
small	**beag** *bug*
hot	**te** *cheh*
cold	**fuar** *fooar*
bigger	**níos mó** *neess mow*
smaller	**níos lú** *neess loo*
hotter	**níos teo** *neess chaw*
colder	**níos fuaire** *neess fooara*
hot water	**uisce te** *ishka cheh*
cold water	**uisce fooar** *ishka fooar*
I am hungry	**tá ocras orm** *taw ukrass uram*
I am thirsty	**tá tart orm** *taw tart uram*
it is cold today	**tá sé fuar inniu** *taw shay fooar inyoo*
it is very warm	**tá sé an-te** *taw shay ann-cheh*
the weather is fine	**tá an aimsir go maith** *taw un Imsher gu mah*
it is cold today	**tá sé fuar inniu** *taw shay fooar inyoo*
isn't it a nice day?	**nach deas an lá é inniu?** *nakh jass un law ay inyoo*
I like weather like this	**is maith liom aimsir mar seo** *iss mah lyum Imsher mar shaw*

do you like tea?	**an maith leat tae?**
	un mah lyat tay
yes, I do	**is maith**
	iss mah
no, I do not	**ní maith**
	nee mah
do you take sugar?	**an ólann tú siúcra?**
	un awlan too shookra
are you hungry?	**an bhfuil ocras ort?**
	un will ukrass urt
yes (I am hungry)	**tá**
	taw
no	**níl**
	neel
are you warm enough?	**an bhfuil tú te go leor?**
	in will too cheh go lyowr
where are we now?	**cá bhfuilimid anois?**
	ka willimij anish
what is that?	**cad é sin?**
	kajay shin
where is it?	**cá bhfuil sé?**
	ka will shay
how do you say?	**cad é mar déarfá?**
	kajay mar jerrha
what is your name?	**cad is ainm duit?**
	kad iss anyim ditch
my name is…	**…is ainm dom**
	…iss anyim dum
switch on the light	**las an solas**
	lass un suliss
put out the light	**cuir as an solas**
	kur iss un suliss
switch on the television	**cuir suas an teilifís**
	kur sooas un tellefish
excuse me	**gabh mo leithscéal**
	gow mu layskal
don't mention it	**ná habhair é**
	naw habber ay
would you like a drink?	**ar mhaith leat deoch?**
	air way lyat jokh
yes (I would)	**ba mhaith**
	ba woy
it does not matter	**is cuma**
	iss kumma
it does not matter to me	**is cuma liom**
	iss kumma lyum

I'm glad to see you	**tá athas orm thú a fheiceáil**
	taw ahass uram hoo eck-al
don't worry	**ná bí buartha**
	haw bee boorha
I feel ill	**mothaím tinn**
	muheeam chinn
I have a cold	**tá slaghdán orm**
	taw slaydan uram
would you like more tea?	**ar mhaith leat tuilleadh tae?**
	air woy lyat chilloo tay
can you drive?	**an féidir leat tiomáint?**
	in fayjar lyat chuminch
everyone	**gach duine**
	gak dinna
everywhere	**gach áit**
	gak itch
almost	**beagnach**
	bugnach
much/many	**a lán/cuid mhór**
	a lann/kuj wore
how many/much?	**cá mhéad**
	ka vayd
somebody	**duine éigin**
	dinna aygin
why (is that)?	**cad chuige (sin)?**
	ka tiga (shin)
turn left here	**gabh ar chlé anseo**
	gow air khlay unshaw
turn right there	**gabh ar dheis ansin**
	gow air yaysh unshin
do you speak Irish?	**an bhfuil Gaeilge agat?**
	un will gaylga ugut
What is your name?	**Cad é an t-ainm atá ort?**
	kajay in tanyim ataw urt
My name is Nora	**Nóra atá orm**
	nora ataw orim

at me	**agam**
	ugum
at you (singular)	**agat**
	ugut
at him	**aige**
	egge
at her	**aice**
	ekee
at us	**againn**
	ugeen
at you (plural)	**agaibh**
	ugiv
at them	**acu**
	akoo

Note the use of the preposition **ag** (at) to imply possession of a thing, e.g. **tá Gaeilge agam** (I have Irish, literally 'Irish is at me'), or **tá cóta agam** (I have a coat).

Days of the week

Sunday	**Dé Domhnaigh**
	je downee
Monday	**Dé Luain**
	je looin
Tuesday	**Dé Máirt**
	je martch
Wednesday	**Dé Céadaoin**
	je kaydeen
Thursday	**Déardaoin**
	jeyrdeen
Friday	**Dé hAoine**
	je haynya
Saturday	**Dé Sathairn**
	je saharn
yesterday	**inné**
	inyay
today	**inniu**
	inyoo
tomorrow	**amárach**
	amawrakh
tonight	**anocht**
	anukht

tomorrow night	**oíche amárach**
	eeha amawrakh
last night	**aréir**
	areyr
where were you last night?	**cá raibh tú aréir?**
	ka row too areyr
I was in the pub	**bhí mé sa teach tábhairne**
	vee may sa chakh tawarnya
where are we going tomorrow?	**cá bhfuilimid ag dul amárach?**
	ka'l mij eg dul amawrakh
we are going to the beach	**táimid ag dul go dtí an trá**
	tamij eg dul gujee in tra
what day is it?	**cad é an lá inniu?**
	kajay in law inyoo
it's Friday	**inniu an Aoine**
	inyoo an aynya
what's the matter?	**cad é tá cearr?**
	kajay taw kyarr
nothing	**rud ar bith**
	rud air bih
help yourself to the milk	**tarraing ort an bainne**
	tarring urt a banya
it cannot be helped	**níl neart air**
	neeil nyart air
I have no choice	**níl an dara suí sa bhuaile agam**
	neeil in dara see sa woolya ugum

(Literally, this means, 'I haven't a second place in the mountain pasture'!)

An Irish proverb

in the land of the blind the one-eyed man is king	**i dtír na ndall is rí fear na leathshúile**
	i jeer na nall iss ree far na lyah-hoola

Parts of the body

head	**ceann**
	kyunn
hair	**gruaig**
	grooag (U),
	grooig (C, M)
your hair	**do chuid gruaige**
	du khuj grooiga
the face	**an aghaidh**
	in I
eye	**súil**
	sooil
the eyes	**na súile**
	na sooila
the nose	**an tsrón**
	in troan
the mouth	**an béal**
	in bell
chin	**smig**
	smig
ear	**cluas**
	klooas
forehead	**éadan**
	eydin
tooth	**fiacail**
	feeakal
teeth	**fiacla**
	feeakla
cheek	**leiceann**
	lekann
throat	**scornach**
	skornakh
shoulder	**gualainn**
	gooalann
shoulder-blade	**slinneán**
	slinyaun
arm	**sciathán**
	skeeahan
elbow	**uillinn**
	ilyinn
hand	**lámh**
	lauw (or *lauv*)
finger	**méar**
	meyr
the fingers	**na méara**
	na meyra

chest	**brollach** (and **cliabh**)
	brulakh (and kleeoow)
stomach	**goile**
	gila
belly	**bolg**
	bulig
waist	**coim**
	kim
leg	**cos** (and **cois**)
	kuss (and kush)
thigh	**más**
	mass
knee	**glúin**
	glooin
calf	**colpa**
	kullepa
ankle	**murnán**
	murnaun

Regular Verbs

stand	**seas**
	shass

Present tense:

I stand	**seasaim**
	shassim
you stand	**seasann tú**
	shassan too
he/she stands	**seasann sé/sí**
	shassan shay/shee
we stand	**seasaimid**
	shassimij
you stand (pl.)	**seasann sibh**
	shassan shiv
they stand	**seasann siad**
	shassan sheead

Past tense:

I stood	**sheas mé**
	hass may
you stood	**sheas tú**
	hass too
he/she stood	**sheas sé/sí**
	hass shay/shee

we stood	**sheasamar**
	hassamar
you (pl.) stood	**sheas sibh**
	hass shiv
they stood	**sheas siad**
	hass sheead

Future tense:

I stand	**seasfaidh mé**
	shass-hee may
you will stand	**seasfaidh tú**
	shass-hee too
he/she will stand	**seasfaidh sé/sí**
	shass-hee shay/shee
we shall stand	**seasfaimid**
	hass-heemij
you will stand (pl.)	**seasfaidh sibh**
	shass-hee shiv
they will stand	**seasfaidh siad**
	shass-hee sheead

Some regular verbs:

move	**bog**
	bug
twist	**cas**
	kass
sell	**díol**
	jeel
praise	**mol**
	mul
take	**glac**
	glak
follow	**lean**
	lan
stop	**stad**
	stad
swim	**snámh**
	snauw (U), snauv (C, M)
write	**scríobh**
	skrioo (U), skreev (C, M)
clean	**glan**
	glan
fill	**líon**
	leen

| raise, build, or take | **tóg** |
| | *taug* |

The Calendar

month	**mí**
	mee
January	**Mí Eanáir**
	mee annar
February	**Mí Feabhra**
	mee fyouwra
March	**Márta**
	marta
April	**Aibreán**
	abran
May	**Mí na Bealtaine**
	mee na baltanya
June	**Meitheamh**
	mehoow
July	**Mí Iúil**
	mee yooil
August	**Mí Lúnasa**
	mee loonassa
September	**Meán Fómhair**
	man fowar
October	**Deireadh Fómhair**
	jerroo fowar
November	**Mí na Samhna**
	mee na souwna
December	**Mí na Nollag**
	mee na nullag

There are numerous alternatives to the names given above; the word **mí** may precede the name, be omitted, or used with the article **an**. There are many variaions, among them:

February	**Mí na bhFaoilleach**
	mee na waeelyakh
June	**Mí mheáin an tSamh-**
	raidh
	mee van a towree
June	**Mí na Féile Eoin**
	mee na feyla owen

July	**Mí na Súl Buí**
	mee na sool bwee

Negative of regular verbs:

stand	**seas**
	shass

Present:

I move	**bogaim**
	bugim
I do not move	**ní bhogaim**
	nee wugim

Past:

I moved	**bhog mé**
	wug may
I did not move	**níor bhog mé**
	neer wug may

Future:

I shall move	**bogfaidh mé**
	bug-hee may
I shall not move	**ní bhogfaidh mé**
	nee wug-hee may

To ask a question:

Place *an* before the verb in the present and future tenses, and *ar* in the past tense. For example:

break	**bris**
	brish
do they break?	**an mbriseann siad?**
	un mrishin sheead
will they break?	**an mbrisfidh siad?**
	un mrish-hee sheead
did they break?	**ar bhris siad?**
	air vrish sheead
did you break it?	**ar bhris tú é?**
	air vrish too ay

Note that *b* is eclipsed by *an*, i.e. *mb* and *b* is not heard, *ar* aspirates the *b*, and it now sounds like *v* (or *w* if used with a broad vowel).

When a verb begins with a vowel or with *f*, it is prefixed by *d* in the past tense. For example:

I drink	**ólaim**
	aulim
I drank	**d'ól mé**
	daul may
he waits	**fanann sé**
	fanin shay
he waited	**d'fhan sé**
	dan shay

Telling the time

what time is it?	**cad é an t-am e?**
	kaday in tam
it is one o'clock	**tá sé a haon a chlog**
	taw shay a hayn a khlug
it is two o'clock	**tá sé a dó a chlog**
	taw shay a dau a khlug
it is half past three	**tá sé leath tar éis a trí**
	taw shay lyah tar esh a tree
after	**tar éis** (C, M) **i ndiaidh** (U)
	tar esh/in yay
it is half past four	**tá sé leath i ndiaidh (or, tar éis) a ceathair**
	taw shay lyah in yay a kehar
it is a quarter past five	**tá sé ceathrú tar éis a cúig**
	taw shay kehroo tar esh a kuig
it is a quarter to six	**tá sé ceathrú go dtí a sé**
	taw shay kehroo go jee a shay
it is twenty past seven	**tá sé fiche i ndiaidh a seacht**
	taw shay fiha in yay a shakht

| it is twenty to eight | **tá sé fiche go dtí a hocht** |
| | *taw shay fiha gu jee a hukht* |

Note the dialectal differences with *after*: **i ndiaidh is more** common in Ulster, while **tar éis** is used in **Munster** and Connacht.

Possessive adjectives:

The possessive pronouns, *mine, yours, his, her, our, their,* do not exist as such in Irish, but the possessive adjective can be used to express the same concept:

my coat	**mo chóta**
	mu khota
your coat	**do chóta**
	du khota
his coat	**a chóta**
	a khota
her coat	**a cóta**
	a kota
our coat	**ár gcóta**
	arr gota
your (pl.) coat	**bhur gcóta**
	wur gota
their coat	**a gcóta**
	a gota

Note that **mo** (my), **do** (your), **a** (his), all aspirate the following noun (provided it begins with a consonant capable of being aspirated). **a** (her), neither aspirates nor eclipses the following noun but prefixes an *h* to any following vowel, e.g. **a hathair** (her father). **a** (their), **bhur** (your *pl.*), **ar** (our) all eclipse the following noun where possible. For example:

their father	**a n-athair**
	a nahar
our father	**ár n-athair**
	arr nahar
your father	**bhur n-athair**
	wur nahar

Conversation

Talking is a popular pastime in Ireland. Here are some terms relating to the art of conversation:

conversation	**comhrá**
	kowra
you are talking nonsense	**tá tú ag glagaireacht**
	taw too eg glagarakht
speaking	**ag labhairt**
	eg lowartch
chattering	**geabaireacht**
	gyabarakht
whisper	**cogar**
	kugar
he whispered to me	**chuir se cogar i mo chluais**
	khur shay kugar i mu khlooish
gossip	**ráfla**
	raffla
I heard a rumour	**chuala me ráfla**
	hula may raffla
tongue-twister	**rabhlóg**
	rouwlog
shout	**scairt**
	skartch
raving	**rámhaille**
	rowalya
scream	**scread**
	skrad
yelling	**béicíl**
	beykeel
he let out a scream	**lig sé beic as**
	lig shay beyk ass
complain	**gearán/clamhsán**
	gyaraun/klouwsaun
backbiting	**cúlchaint**
	koolkhantch
eavesdrop	**cúléist**
	kooleysht
eavesdropper	**cúléisteoir**
	kooleyshtyor
boasting	**ag maíomh**
	eg mweeoo
narrative	**scéalaíocht**
	skeyleeakht

news	**scéala**
	skeyla
story	**scéal**
	skeyl
argument	**argóint**
	arigointch
I saw a good film last night	**chonaic me scannán maith aréir**
	hanik may skanan maith areyr
there is a good film on the television tonight	**tá scannán maith ar an teilifís anocht**
	taw skanan maith air in tellefish anukht

Accomodation and Hotels

hotel	**teach ósta/óstlann**
	chack austa/austlan
we are staying at a hotel	**táimid ag fanacht i dteach ósta**
	tawmij a fanakht i jach usta
send the maid up	**cuir an cailín aimsire aníos chugainn**
	kur in kaleen imshera aneeas hugeen
is there a bathroom on this floor?	**an bhfuil seomra folchtha or an urlár seo?**
	un will shumra fulka air in urlar shaw
towel	**tuáille**
	too-oilya
soap	**gallúnach**
	galoonakh

The churches frequently hold services in Irish when and where appropriate. Anyone attending these should try to obtain the printed texts to be used, which are often readily available.

the church	**an Eaglais** *in aglish*
chapel	**teach an phobail** *chakh a fubal*
Mass	**aifreann** *affrin*
church service	**seirbhís eaglasta** *shervish aglasta*
The Church of Ireland	**Eaglais na hÉireann** *aglish na heyrann*
the priest	**an sagart** *in saggart*
the minister	**an ministir** *in minishter*

---

do you have any rooms free?	**an bhfuil aon seomra saor agat?** *un will aen shomrah seer ugut?*
I'd like a room…	**ba mhaith liom seomra…** *bah waih lyum shom-rah…*
with a double bed	**le leaba dhúbailte** *leh lyaba dhoobal-tche*
with twin beds	**le dhá leaba** *leh ghaa lyabah*
with a bathroom	**le seomra folctha** *leh shomrah folk-ha*
with a nice view	**le radharc deas** *leh rowark jass*
at the front	**ag an tosach** *eg un tussahh*
at the back	**ar chúl** *er khool*
we will be staying…	**beimid ag fanacht…** *bay mij eg fanakht*
overnight	**thar oíche** *har eeha*
a couple of days	**cúpla lá** *koopla la*
a week	**ar feadh seachtaine** *er fow shahhtenya*

a fortnight	**ar feadh coicíse**
	er fow kukisha
perhaps	**b'fhéidir**
	bay-jer
may I see the room	**an féidir liom an seomra a fheiceáil**
	un fey jer lyum a shom-rah ah ekoyl
I don't like it	**ní maith liom é**
	nee maih lyum ay
it is...	**tá sé...**
	tau shay
too small	**ró bheag**
	roh vug
too cold	**ró fhuar**
	roh uar
too dark	**ró dhorcha**
	roh ghor ahha
too noisy	**ró challánach**
	roh hhallanahh
too dirty	**ró shalach**
	roh halakh
give me	**tabhair dom**
	tawer dum
give me a bigger room	**tabhair dom seomra níos mó**
	tawer dum shomrah nees mo

Food

bread	**arán**
	arann
toast	**arán rósta**
	arann rawsta
brown bread	**arán donn**
	arann dunn
potato bread	**arán prátí**
	arann pratee
wheaten bread	**arán cruithneachta**
	arann krihnakhta
oaten bread	**arán coirce**
	arann kur-ka
salt	**salann**
	salan

pepper	**piobar**
	pibbar
garlic	**gairleog**
	garlyog
sea salt	**salann sáile**
	salan soyl-a
meat	**feoil**
	fyawil
mutton	**caoireoil**
	keeryawil
bacon	**bagún**
	bagoon
pork	**muiceoil**
	mukyawil
beef	**feoil mhairt**
	fyawil wartch
sausage	**ispín**
	ishpeen
sausages	**ispíní**
	ishpeenee
potatoes	**prátaí**
	pratee

Garlic was never very popular in Irish cooking, but still is well known and widely available. It was once fed to cattle and other livestock to protect them from disease as its medical properties were highly regarded by country people. Its main use among the Irish population, therefore, was medicinal. It is still taken as a medicine in some areas during epidemics of cold and 'flu.

sugar	**siúcra**
	shookra
egg	**ubh**
	iv
eggs	**uibheacha**
	ivakha
boiled egg	**ubh bhruite**
	iv vritcha
fried eggs	**uibheacha friochta**
	ivakha frikhta

scrambled eggs	**uibheacha scrofa**
	ivakha skrufa
a raw egg	**ubh amh**
	iv auw
tea	**tae**
	tay
coffee	**caife**
	kafee
milk	**bainne**
	banya
goat's milk	**bainne gabhair**
	banya gowayr
buttermilk	**bláthach**
	bla-akh
cheese	**cáis** (C, M), **cáise** (U)
	kaash (C,M), *kaashee* (U)
butter	**im**
	imm
home-made butter	**im baile**
	im bala
fish	**iasc** (*plural:* **éisc**)
	eeask (ayshk)
trout	**breac** (*plural:* **bric**)
	brak (brik)
sea trout	**brak geal**
	brak gyal
salmon	**bradán** (pl: **bradáin**)
	braddan (bradoin)
mackerel	**murlas**
	murlass
cod	**trosc**
	trusk
herrings	**scadán**
	skaddan
mussels	**sliogáin dhubha**
	sligoyn goow-a
or	**diúilicíní**
	joolikeenee
oysters	**oisrí**
	ushree
crab	**portán**
	purtann
lobster	**gliomach**
	glimmakh
chicken	**sicín**
	shikeen

soup	**anraith**
	anreeh
vegetable soup	**anraith glasraí**
	anreeh glassree
onions	**oinniúin**
	unyoowin
sauce	**anlann**
	annlann

An Irish saying:

| Hunger is good sauce | **Is maith an t-anlann an t-ocras** |
| | *iss moih an tannlann un tukrass* |

---

tomatoes	**trátaí**
	traatee
beans	**pónairí**
	pownaree
carrot	**meacan dearg**
	mekan jareg
beetroot	**biatas**
	beeatass
parsnips	**meacan bán**
	mekan bawn

Another regular verb:

| dwell | **cónaigh** |
| | *konee* |

Present tense:

I dwell	**cónaím**
	koneeim
you dwell	**cónaíonn tú**
	koneean too
he/she dwells	**cónaíonn sé/sí**
	koneean shay/shee
we dwell	**cónaímid**
	koneeimij
you dwell	**cónaíonn sibh**
	koneean shiv
they dwell	**cónaíonn siad**
	koneean sheead

Past tense:

I dwelt	**chónaigh mé**	*khonee may*
you dwelt	**chónaigh tú**	*khonee too*
he/she dwelt	**chónaigh sé/sí**	*khonee shay/shee*
we dwelt	**chónaíomar**	*khoneeamar*
you dwelt	**chónaigh sibh**	*khonee shiv*
they dwelt	**chónaigh siad**	*khonee sheead*

Future tense:

I shall dwell	**cónóidh mé**	*kono-ee may*
you will dwell	**cónóidh tú**	*kono-ee too*
he/she will dwell	**cónóidh sé/sí**	*kono-ee shay/shee*
we shall dwell	**cónóimid**	*kono-eemij*
you will dwell	**cónóidh sibh**	*kono-ee shiv*
they will dwell	**cónóidh siad**	*kono-ee sheead*

The following are similarly conjugated:

buy	**ceannaigh**	*kyanee*
ask	**fiafraigh**	*feefree*
search	**cuardaigh**	*kooardee*
arrange	**socraigh**	*sukree*
begin	**tosaigh**	*tusee*
examine	**scrúdaigh**	*skroodee*
paint	**dathaigh**	*dahee*
satisfy	**sásaigh**	*sausee*
cover	**clúdaigh**	*kloodee*

protect	**cumhdaigh**
	koowdoo

I prefer	**is fearr liom**
	iss farr lyum
I prefer tea to coffee	**is fearr liom tae ná caife**
	iss farr lyum tay na kafee
I don't like carrots	**ní maith liom meacan dearg**
	nee moih lyum mekan jareg
I like potatoes	**is maith liom prátaí**
	iss moih lyum pratee
do you like milk?	**an maith leat bainne?**
	un moih lyat banya
yes, I do, but I prefer cream	**is maith, ach is fearr liom uachtar**
	iss moih akh iss farr lyum ooakhter
which do you prefer, tea or coffee?	**cé acu is fearr leat: tae nó caife?**
	kay akoo iss farr lyat tay no kafee
would you prefer coffee?	**arbh fhearr leat caife?**
	airiv arr lyat kafee
yes, I would	**b'fhearr**
	barr
would you like more?	**ar mhaith leat tuilleadh?**
	air woih lyat chilyoo
no, thank you	**níor mhaith, go raibh maith agat**
	neer woih gurra moih ugut
she prefers carrots to parsnips	**Is fearr léi meacan dearg ná meacan bán**
	iss farr layhe mekan jareg na mekan bawn
pass me the salt please	**chuir chugam an sal- ann le do thoil**
	khur hugim un salan le du huyl

with me	**liom**
	lyum
with you	**leat**
	lyat
with him	**leis**
	laysh
with her	**léi**
	layhe
with us	**linn**
	ling
with you	**libh**
	liv
with them	**leo**
	law

I would like some bread	**ba mhaith liom giota aráin**
	bu woih lyum gita aroin
do you take sugar?	**an ólann tú siúcra?**
	un awlin too shookra
I do/I don't	**ólaim/ní ólaim**
	awlim/nee awlim
(yes) I am	**tá**
	taw
(no) I am not	**níl**
	nee-il

There is no word for *yes* or *no* in Irish as in English. One simply uses the positive or negative form of the verb used in the question, as in the examples above.

the trout is very tasty	**tá an breac an-bhlasta**
	taw un brak ann-vlasta
the salmon is tasty too	**tá an bradán blasta freisin**
	taw un braddan blasta freshin
have you enough?	**an bhfuil go leor agat?**
	un will gu lyowr ugut

I have had enough	**tá mo sháith agam** *taw mu hlh ugum*
thank you	**go raibh maith agat** *gurra moih ugut*
please	**le do thoil** *le du huyl*
don't mention it	**ná habair é** *na habber ay*
is there any more fish?	**an bhfuil tuilleadh éisc ann?** *un will tilyoo ayshk unn*
red wine	**fíon dearg** *feen jareg*
white wine	**fíon bán** *feen bawn*
cutlery	**sceanra** *skyanra*
do you have…?	**an bhfuil…agat?** *un will…ugut*
I am hungry	**tá ocras orm** *taw ukrass uram*

on me	**orm** *uram*
on you	**ort** *urt*
on him	**air** *air*
on her	**uirthi** *urhee*
on us	**orainn** *ureen*
on you	**oraibh** *uriv*
on them	**orthu** *urha*

what do you recommend?	**cad é a mholann tú** *kajay a wullen too*
there is too much salt in it	**ta barraíocht salainn ann** *taw bareeakht saloin ann*

a meal	**béile**
	beyla
meals	**béilí**
	beylee
dinner	**dinnéar**
	dinyayr
breakfast	**bricfeasta**
	brikfesta
lunch	**lón**
	loan
restaurant	**teach itheacháin/ proinnteach**
	chakh ihakhoin/ princhakh

Travel

car	**carr**
	karr
coach	**cóiste**
	koshtcha
aeroplane	**eitleán**
	etchilan
ship	**long**
	lung
boat	**bád**
	bawd
bicycle	**rothar**
	ruhar
driving	**ag tiomáint**
	a tchumantch
driving a car	**ag tiomáint cairr**
	a tchumantch ka-yr
driver	**tiománaí**
	tchumanee
who is the driver?	**cé hé an tiománaí?**
	kay hay in tchumanee
(the) road	**(an) bothar**
	in bowhar
throroughfare (or route)	**bealach**
	balakh
flying	**ag eitilt**
	eg etchiltch
flight	**eitilt**
	etchiltch

airport	**aerfort**
	airfurt
how do you get to the airport from here?	**cad é an bealach go dtí an t-aerfort as seo?**
	kajay in balakh gujee in tairfurt ass shau
landing (by ship)	**teacht i dtír**
	chakht i jeer
landing (by plane)	**(ag) tuirlingt**
	turlingtch
I came by plane	**tháinig mé ar an eitleán**
	hanig may air in etchilan
runway	**rúidbhealach**
	rooj-valakh
the plane landed on the runway	**thuirling an t-eitleán ar an rúidbhealach**
	hurling in tetchilan air in rooj-valakh
jetplane	**scairdeitleán**
	skarj-etchilan
crossroads	**crosbhóthar**
	krusswowhar
a trip	**turas**
	turiss
a walk	**siúlóid**
	shooloyj
walking	**ag siúl**
	eg shool
going for a walk	**dul ar siúlóid**
	dul air shooloyj
rambling	**ag spaisteoireacht**
	a spashchorakht
will you take me to the station please?	**an dtabharfaidh tú chuig an stáisiún mé, le do thoil**
	in dawrhee too hig in stashoon may, le du huyl
what is the fare?	**cád é an táille?**
	kajay in tal-ya
two pounds	**dhá phunt**
	gaw funt

where is the booking office?	**cá bhfuil an oifig ticéad?** *ka'l in ifig chikeyd*
enquiries office	**oifig faisnéise** *ifig fashnesha*
platform three	**ardán a trí** *ardan a tree*
luggage	**bagáiste** *bagoishta*
waiting room	**feithealann** *fehalann*
where do you get the train to Dublin?	**cá bhfaigheann tú an traein go Baile Átha Cliath?** *ka wlyen too in treyn gu bala kleea*
when is the next train?	**cá huair a bheidh an chéad traein eile ann?** *ka hoor a bay in kheydt reyn ella unn*
the first train	**an chéad traein** *in kheyd treyn*
the next train	**an chéad traein eile** *in kheyd treyn ella*
the last train	**an traein dheireanach** *in treyn yeranakh*

Most main cities and towns in Ireland can be reached by an arterial rail network with its centre in Dublin, otherwise the provincial bus service can be used. The latter primarily serves rural areas, and short journeys by bus through Irish-speaking districts provide useful opportunities for hearing the language spoken.

---

does the train stop at Athlone?	**an stadann an traein ag Áth Luain?** *un staden in treyn eg ah looin*
yes (it does stop)	**stadann** *staden*
no (it does not stop)	**ní stadann** *nee staden*

what is the quickest way to get to Galway?	**cad é an bealach is giorra go Gaillimh?** *kajay in balakh iss gyurra gu galyiv*
I walked to the house	**shiúil mé go dtí an teach** *hyooil may gujee in chakh*
where is the beach?	**cá bhfuil an trá?** *ka'l in traw*
it's down there	**tá thíos ansin** *taw hees unshin*
is it far?	**an bhfuil sé i bhfad?** *un will shay i wad*
yes, it is two miles	**tá, tá sé dhá mhíle slí** *taw, taw shay gaw veela slee*
how did you get here?	**cén bealach a tháimig tú?** *keyen balakh a hanig too*
I came over the hill	**tháinig mé thar an chnoc** *hanig may har a kh-nuk*
I took a shortcut	**ghearr mé an t-aicearra** *yar may in tekera*
the sea-shore	**an cladach** *in kladakh*
the beach	**an trá** *in traw (C, M) in trl (U)*
the sea	**an fharraige** *in arriga*
sailing	**ag seoladh** *eg shawloo*
sailing boat	**bád seolta** *bawd shawlta*
lake	**loch** *lokh*
mountain	**sliabh** *sleev (C, M) sleeoo (U)*
the mountains	**na sléibhte** *na slevtche*
hill	**cnoc** *k-nuk (C, M) kruk (U)*

the hills	**na cnoic** *na k-nik (C, M) na krik (U)*
a beautiful view	**radharc álainn** *rawark auleen*
sunset	**luí gréine** *lee greynya*
the sun	**an ghrian** *in ghreean*
beautiful	**álainn** (or **go hálainn**) *auleen (gu hauleen)*
it is beautiful	**tá sé go hálainn** *taw shay gu hauleen*
is there anything to see around here?	**an bhfuil rud ar bith le feiceáil thart anseo?** *un will rud er bih le fekoil hart unshaw*
yes, a lot	**tá, cuid mhór** *taw, kuj wore*
for example	**mar shampla** *mar hampla*
there is a castle near this place	**tá caisleán in aice leis an áit seo** *taw kashlan in eka lesh in Itch shaw*
a standing stone	**gallán** (or **liagán**) *galawn (leeagawn)*
a rath	**ráth** *rah*
monastery	**mainistir** *manishter*
round tower	**túr cruinn** *toor krin*
museum	**iarsmalan** (or **músaem**) *eersmalan (moosaym)*
archaeology	**seandálaíocht** *shandaleeakht*
archaeological remains	**iarsmaí seandálaíochta** *eersmee shandaleeakhta*

Many types of archaeological survivals can be found all over Ireland. Forts, souterrains, crannogs, towers, megalithic tombs, standing stones, stone circles, burial mounds and all manner of interesting antiquities literally dot the countryside. They are easily found, especially on O.S. maps, and information about them is readily available (see, for example, *Outings in Ireland* by Hugh Oram, Appletree Press, 1982).

---

up in the mountains	**thuas sna sléibhte**
	hooass sna slevtcha
down in the glen	**thíos sa ghleann**
	heess sa ghlann
among the trees	**i measc na gcrann**
	i mask na gran
the leaves on the trees	**na duilleoga ar na crainn**
	na dilyoga air na krin
a bird in the sky	**éan thuas sa spéir**
	eyan hooass sa speyr
out on the lake	**amuigh ar an loch**
	amwee air in lokh
are there many fish in the river?	**an bhfuil mórán iasc san abhainn?**
	un will moran eeask san owen
I don't know	**níl a fhios agam**
	neeil'iss ugum

---

wonderful	**go hiontach**
	gu heentakh
impressive	**suntasach**
	suntasakh
peaceful	**suaimhneach**
	sooivnyakh
superb	**ar fheabhas**
	air owas
strange	**aisteach**
	Ishchakh
quiet	**ciúin**
	kyooin
interesting	**suimiúil**
	simiooil
tremendous	**millteanach**
	milchanakh
ostentatious	**taibhseach**
	tIvshakh

Sports

football	**peil** *pell*
playing football	**ag imirt peile** *eg imertch pella*
where is the ball?	**cá bhfuil an liathróid?** *ka'l in leeahroij*
it is in the long grass	**tá sí san fhéar fada** *taw shee san yeyr fada*
we've lost it	**tá sí caillte againn** *taw shee klltcha ugeen*
a game of football	**cluiche peile** *kliha pella*
who do you think will win?	**cé a bhainfidh an cluiche i do bharúil?** *kay a winhee a kliha i du warooil*
it's hard to tell	**is doiligh a rá** *iss dilee a raw*
it will be a draw	**beidh sé cothrom** *bay shay kuhrum*
team	**foireann** *furann*
the teams	**na foirne** *na furnya*
golf	**galf** *galf*
golf course	**galfchúrsa** *galfkhoorsa*
what were you doing?	**cad é bhí sibh a dhéanamh?** *kaday vee shiv a yanoo*
we were playing golf	**bhímid ag imirt gailf** *veemij eg emertch galf*
can you swim?	**an bhfuil snámh agat?** *un will snouw ugut*
is there a swimming pool near here?	**an bhfuil linn snámha in aice leis seo?** *un will linn snouwa in eka lesh seo*
swimming pool	**linn snámha** *linn snava (C, M),* *snouwa (U)*

the sea is too cold for swimming	**tá an fharraige rófhuar le haghaidh snámha**
	taw in ariga rau-oor le hl snouwa
hurling	**iománaíocht**
	umauneeakht
hurling stick	**camán**
	kamaun

Gaelic football, **peil Ghaelach**, is the most popular Celtic game in Ireland, closely followed by hurling, **iománaíocht**. Hurling is a fast exciting game but can be dangerous if played without training. Protective headgear is now common and serious injury is comparatively rare. **Camógaíocht**, or camogie, is similar to hurling, and played by women.

---

goal	**cúl**
	kool
the referee	**an réiteoir**
	in reytchor
cycling	**rothaíocht**
	ruheeakht
bicycle	**rothar**
	ruhar
wheel	**roth**
	ruh
the brakes	**na coscáin**
	na kuskoin
where can I hire a bike?	**cá háit a bhfuil rothar le fáil ar cíos**
	ka hltch a will ruhar le foil air khees
I have a puncture	**tá poll sa roth agam**
	taw pul sa ruh ugum
pedal	**troitheán**
	treehan
there are too many hills	**tá barraíocht cnoc ann**
	taw bareakht kruk unn
let's go for a walk	**téimis amach ar shiúlóid**
	tcheyimish amakh air hyooloij

climbing	**dreapadóireacht**
	drapadorakht
sailing	**ag seoladh**
	eg shauloo
sailing boat	**bád seoil**
	bawd shawil
hooker	**pucan**
	pukawn
sail	**seol**
	shaul
mast	**crann**
	kran
the rudder	**an stiúir**
	in styoor
there is a good wind for sailing today	**tá gaoth mhaith sheolta ann inniu**
	taw gee woih hyawlta unn inyoo
horse riding	**marcaíocht**
	markeeakht
horse	**capall**
	kapal
saddle	**diallait**
	jeealitch
my horse has no saddle	**níl diallait ar mo chapall**
	neeil jeealitch air mu khapal
sun-bathing	**ag déanamh bolg le gréin**
	eg janoo bulig le greyn
sunny weather	**aimsir ghréine**
	Imsher ghreynya
fine weather	**aimsir mhaith**
	Imsher woih

Drinking

in the pub	**sa teach tábhairne**
	sa chakh tawarnya
a drink	**deoch**
	jukh
drinking	**ag ól**
	eg aul
what would you like to drink?	**cad é ba mhaith leat le hól?**
	kaday ba mhaith leat le haul

I would like a glass of beer	**ba mhaith liom gloine leanna** *bu woih lyum glinya lanna*
beer	**leann/beoir** *lann/byor*
a pint of beer	**pionta leanna** *pinnta lanna*
cider	**fíon úll/ceirtlis** *feen ool/kyertlish*
wine	**fíon** *feen*
vermouth	**fíon mormónta** *feen morimonta*
whiskey	**uisce beatha** *ishka baha*
spirits	**biotáille** *bitoilya*

The word 'whiskey' comes originally from Irish **uisce beatha**, literally 'the water of life'. The word has re-entered the language in some areas as **fuisce** (*fwishka*), more common in Connacht than elsewhere, and **uisce beatha** is still the more common form of the word. **Poitín** (*potcheen*) is the word for home-made whiskey. **Poitín** is made in almost all parts of Ireland, but it has a particularly strong association with Gaeltacht areas. It can be made from potatoes but also from numerous vegetable products, always to a traditional recipe. Its taste tends towards a certain roughness, especially to the unaccustomed drinker, and there are a number of cocktails available. Anything mixed with **poitín** is called a **manglam** (especially in Connemara). **Poitín** must be taken with caution as its effects can be devastating. In any case making it is an offence, with severe penalties! (For a light-hearted history, see *In Praise of Poteen* by John McGuffin, Appletree Press).

give me two pints of beer please	**tabhair dom dhá phionta leanna le do thoil** *tawar dum gau finnta lanna, le du hul*

the same again	**an rud céanna arís** *in rud keyna arish*
this is my round	**seo mo sheal** *shaw mu hyall*
or	**seal s' agamsa** *shall sugumsa*
would you like another one?	**ar mhaith leat ceann eile?** *air woih lyat kyunn ella*
yes (I would)	**ba mhaith** *bu woih*
no (I would not)	**níor mhaith** *neer woih*
would you like a cigarette?	**ar mhaith leat toitín?** *air woih lyat tutcheen*
he is drunk	**tá sé ar meisce** *taw shay air meyshka*

There are various degrees of inebriation. Here are the Irish words for a few of them:

drunk	**ar meisce** *air meyshka*
very drunk	**ar deargmheisce** *air jaregveyshka*
quite drunk	**ólta** *aulta*
'blind drunk'	**caoch ólta** *kayokh aulta*
tipsy	**súgach** *soogakh*

---

have a drink	**bíodh deoch agat** *beeoo jukh ugut*
wine divulges truth (in vino veritas)	**scilidh fíon fírinne** *skilee feen feerinya*
drink it up and don't let it come back	**caith siar é agus ná lig aniar é** *klh sheer ay ugus na lig anyeer ay*
wine is sweet but paying for it is bitter	**is milis fíon, ach is searbh a íoc** *iss milish feen akh iss sharoo a eek*

one for the road	**deoch an dorais**
	jukh a darish
late drinking	**ragairne**
	ragarnya
to go on a spree of revelry and debauchery	**dul chun drabhláis**
	dul hun drowlish
we went on a spree last night	**chuaigh muid ar na canaí aréir**
	hooee mij air na kanee areyr
cheers (health)	**sláinte**
	slauntcha
sober	**stuama**
	stooama
sobriety	**stuaim**
	stooim
do you take an occasional drink?	**an ólann tú corrdheoch?**
	un aulan too koryukh

Games

(he is) playing cards	**ag imirt cartaí**
	eg imertch cartee
hearts	**hart** (pl. **hairt**)
	hart (pl. *hartch*)
diamonds	**muileata** (pl. **muileataí**)
	mwilata (pl. *mwilatee*)
spades	**spéireata** (pl. **spéireataí**)
	speyrata (pl. *speyratee*)
clubs	**triuf** (pl. **triufanna**)
	truf (pl. *trufanna*)
the ace	**an t-aon**
	in tayn
the jack	**an cuireata**
	in kurata
the queen	**an bhanríon**
	in wanreean
the king	**an rí**
	in ree
the king of hearts	**an rí hairt**
	in ree hartch

trump	**mámh** *maw*
a game	**cluiche** *kliha*
twenty fives	**cúig is fiche** *kooig iss fiha*
chess	**ficheall** *fihall*
draughts	**táiplis** *taplish*
backgammon	**táiplis mhór** *taplish wore*
chess-board	**clár fichille** *klar fihilya*
chess pieces	**foireann fichille** *furan fihilya*
pawn	**giolla** (or **ceithearnach**) *gilla (or kehernakh)*
the king	**an rí** *in ree*
the queen	**an bhanríon** *in wanreean*
the bishop	**an tEaspag** *in chaspug*
the knight	**an ridire** *in rijera*
the rook	**an caisleán** *in kashlan*
check	**sáinn** *slnn*
in check	**i sáinn** *i slnn*
checkmate	**marbhsháinn** *maroohlnn*
stalemate	**leamhsháinn** *lyouwhlnn*

Chess, backgammon and similar board games have been played in Ireland since pre-christian times. They are referred to in the sagas and folk-tales and there is nearly always some ritual or allegorical purpose attached to them. Proficiency at chess was also reputed to be a requirement of the ancient warrior caste, the *Fianna*.

Fishing

fishing	**iascaireacht**
	eeaskarakht
I went fishing	**chuaigh mé a iascaireacht**
	khoowee may a eeaskarakht
how is the fishing here?	**cad é mar atá an iascaireacht anseo?**
	kajay mar ataw in eeaskarakht unshaw
it is good	**tá go maith**
	taw gu moih
it is bad	**tá go dona**
	taw gu dunna
it is fairly good	**tá sé go measartha**
	taw shay gu massarha
fishing rod	**slat iascaireachta**
	slat eeaskarakhta
fishing line	**ruaim**
	rooim
fishing hook	**duán**
	dooaun
waders	**buataisí uisce**
	booatishee ishka
to catch a fish	**iasc a cheapadh**
	eeask a khapoo
I caught a salmon	**mharaigh mé bradán**
	waree may braddan
I didn't catch a thing	**níor mharaigh mé rud ar bith**
	neer waree may rud air bih
bait	**baoite**
	bweetcha
flies	**cuileoga**
	kilyoga
worms	**péisteanna**
	peyshtanna
fly-fishing	**iascaireacht chuil**
	eeaskarakht khil
a fish	**iasc**
	eeask
the fish	**an t-iasc**
	in cheeask

can I fish in this river?	**an bhfuil cead agam iascaireacht a dhéanamh san abhainn seo?**
	un will kad ugum eeaskarakht a yanoo san owen shaw
salmon	**bradán**
	braddan
trout	**breac** (pl. **bric**)
	brak (pl. *brik*)
sea trout	**breac geal**
	brak gyal
sea fishing	**iascaireacht mhara**
	eeaskarakht warra
fisherman	**iascaire**
	eeaskara
going to sea	**dul chun na farraige**
	dul hun na fariga
swimming	**ag snámh**
	ag snauv

When addressing someone in Irish, the vocative case is used. This involves placing a before the person's name and, in some cases, aspirating the first letter. Here are a few examples:

Seán (John)	**'A Sheáin'**
	a hyann
Máire (Mary)	**'A Mháire'**
	a wlra
Cairde (friends)	**'A chairde'**
	a kharja
Fir (men)	**'A fheara'**
	a arra
Pádraig (Patrick)	**'A Phádraig'**
	a fawdrig
Séamas (James)	**'A Shéamais'**
	a heymish
Liam (William)	**'A Liam'**
	a leeam
Bean (woman)	**'A bhean'**
	a van
Tomás (Thomas)	**'A Thomáis'**
	a homish

| 'Be quiet, children' | **'Ciúnas a pháistí'**
kyoonass a fawshtee |

Music

music	**ceol** *kyaul*
do you like music?	**an maith leat an ceol?** *un moih lyat an kyaul*
yes (I do)	**is maith** *iss moih*
no (I don't)	**ní maith** *nee moih*
I don't really care	**is cuma liom** *iss kuma lyum*
I don't mind it	**ní miste liom é** *nee mishtcha lyum ay*
traditional music	**ceol traidisiúnta** *kyaul tradishoonta*
playing music	**ag seinm ceoil** *eg shenyim kyoil*
can you play?	**an féidir leat seinm?** *un feyjer lyat shenyim*
you played it well	**sheinn tú go maith é** *heyn too gu moih ay*
entertainment (musical)	**siamsa** *sheeamsa*
he is playing well	**tá sé ag seinm go maith** *taw shay eg shenyim gu moih*
the fiddle/violin	**an fhidil** *in ijil*
the fiddle is my favourite instrument	**an fhidil an gléas is ansa liom** *in ijil in gless iss ansa lyum*
which is your favourite instrument?	**cén gléas is fearr leat?** *kay akoo gless iss fearr lyat*
a musical instrument	**gléas ceoil** *gless kyoil*

the Irish pipes	**an phíb**
	in feeb

(Also called *uillean pipes* because they are pumped by a bellows under the arm.)

Scottish bagpipes	**píob mhór**
	peeb wore
piping	**píobaireacht**
	peebarakht
those pipes are out of tune	**tá an phíob sin as gléas**
	taw in feeb shin ass gless
accordion	**bosca ceoil**
	buska kyoil
what sort of tune is that?	**cad é an cineál poirt é sin?**
	kaday in kinyal portch ay shin
it's a hornpipe	**cornphíopa atá ann**
	kornfeepa ataw unn
play a jig	**buail suas port**
	booil sooass purt

(The word **port** can also mean 'a tune'.)

jigs (or tunes)	**poirt**
	portch
reels	**ríleanna**
	reelanna

Traditional Irish music is as popular today as ever, and is widely available on records, etc. 'Sessions' of Irish music are common, and there are a number of professional players. Most musicians are amateurs, however, and come from a large cross-section of the population. The music is based on a native 'modal' system which gives it its characteristic flavour. It also has its own system of ornamentation and accents which give it its so-called 'lilt'.

---

drum	**bodhrán**
	bowran
concertina	**consairtín**
	kunsarteen
bravo!	**maith thú**
	moih hoo

song	**amhrán**
	awraun
singer	**amhránaí**
	awraunee
he is a good singer (or player)	**is maith an ceoltóir é**
	iss moih in kyaultor ay
that's a nice song	**sin amhrán deas**
	shin awraun jass
dancing	**rince** (C, M) **damhsa** (U)
	rinka, dowsa
that girl is a fine dancer	**is breá an rinceoir an cailín sin**
	iss braw in rinkyor in kaleenshin
will there be any music tonight?	**an mbeidh aon cheol ann anocht?**
	un may ayn khyaul unn anukht
yes (there will be)	**beidh**
	bay
no (there will not be)	**ní bheidh**
	nee vay
there was a good 'session' in the pub last night	**bhí seisiún maith sa teach tábhairne aréir**
	vee seshoon moih sa chakh tawarnya areyr
there were a lot of musicians playing there	**bhí a lán ceoltóirí ag seinm ansin**
	vee a lawn kyaultoree eg shenyim unshin
how many fiddlers were there?	**cá mhéad fidléir a bhí ann?**
	ka veyd fijiler a vee unn
three fiddlers	**triúr fidléir**
	troor fijiler
no fiddlers	**fidléir ar bith**
	fijiler air bih
tin whistle	**feadóg**
	feejog
flute	**feadóg mhór**
	fadog wore
flute music	**ceol na feadóige**
	kyaul na fadoiga

what did you think of the music?	**cad é a shíl tú den cheol?**
	kajay a heel too din khyaul
I didn't enjoy it	**níor thaitin sé liom**
	neer hatchin shay lyum
it was fine	**bhí sé go breá**
	vee shay gu braw
it was average	**bhí sé go measartha**
	vee shay gu massarha
it was terrible	**bhí sé go holc**
	veeshay gu hulk
sweet music	**ceol binn**
	kyaul binn
harmonious	**binn**
	binn

Shopping

buying things	**ag ceannach rudaí**
	a kyanakh rudee
goods	**earraí**
	arree
supermarket	**sármhargadh**
	sarwaragoo
a good bargain	**margadh maith**
	maragoo moih
you got a good bargain there	**fuair tú margadh maith ansin**
	foor too maragoo moih ansin
what price is it?	**cad é an luach atá air?**
	kajay in luach ata air
how much is it?	**cá mhéad sin?**
	kaveyd shin
it is five pounds	**cúig phunt atá air**
	kooig funt ataw air
it's too dear	**tá sé ródhaor**
	taw shay raugeer
give me something else	**tabhair dom rud éigin eile**
	tawar dum rud eygin ella
show me another one	**taispeáin ceann eile dom**
	tashpan kyunn ella dom

I don't like this one	**ní maith liom an ceann seo**
	nee moih lyum in kyunn shaw
I prefer this one	**is fearr liom an ceann seo**
	iss farr lyum in kyunn shaw
a clothes shop	**siopa éadaí**
	shuppa eydee
where can I buy sweets?	**cá háit arbh fhéidir liom milseáin a cheannach?**
	ka hltch erivejer lyum milshoin a kyanakh
I don't like the colour of it	**ní maith liom an dath atá air**
	nee moih lyum in dah ataw air
what did you buy?	**cad é a cheannaigh tú?**
	kajay a khyanee too
nothing	**rud ar bith**
	rud air bih

Éire

The areas where Irish is regularly spoken are known as **An Ghaeltacht** and are shown by black shading.